elementary vector geometry

elementary vector geometry

seymour schuster

associate professor of mathematics

carleton college, northfield, minnesota

john wiley and sons, inc.

new york   london

Library of Congress Catalog Card Number: 62-10933
Printed in the United States of America

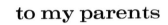

to my parents

preface

This short work is the outgrowth of lectures that were presented at a National Science Foundation Institute held at Carleton College in the summer of 1959. The lectures were to serve the purpose of "enriching" the backgrounds of geometry teachers. However, the pattern of events in mathematics education indicates that the material covered is no longer enrichment material but, rather, essential knowledge for every teacher.

It was just a few years ago that linear algebra was a course for beginning graduate students and vector analysis was typically taken as an upper class course by mathematics, physics, and engineering students. The last decade has brought a revolution in undergraduate mathematics education, and today the knowledge of vectors is acquired at a much earlier stage. Indeed, it is quite usual for college freshmen to study vectors and matrices, particularly as applied to geometry. Furthermore, the studies and recommendations made by the

Commission on Mathematics, the School Mathematics
Study Group, and the Committee on the Undergraduate
Program in Mathematics all point in the direction of
getting some of these concepts into the high school
curriculum. I have long felt that vector techniques
should and will find their way into the high school
curriculum—perhaps not as an integral part of the mathematical training of all students but, at the very least, as
work to excite and challenge superior students.

On a very elementary level, this textbook deals primarily with the development of vector algebra as a
mathematical tool in geometry. The aim is to gain a
greater insight into the theorems by attempting vector
proofs and analytic proofs in contrast to the synthetic
proofs, a knowledge of which the reader brings as a
prerequisite. The elements of vector algebra are developed slowly—more so than in any of the standard works
on vectors. Simple geometric explanations, as well as
numerous illustrations, are used. Beyond this, some
analytic geometry (in two and three dimensions) is
developed as a natural outgrowth of the vector treatment.
In addition, the vector approach is used to assist in other
areas of elementary mathematics: algebra, trigonometry
(plane and spherical), and higher geometry. In short,
vectors have been employed whenever it was felt that
they would aid in gaining insight and/or in facilitating
computations and proofs. I have tried to develop very
little machinery but to go a long way with this small
amount. Accordingly, the reader will find himself
dealing with such topics as linear inequalities, convexity,
linear programming, involutes, and projective theorems.

As for prerequisites, they are not listed formally
because I do not claim to have given a logical (axiomatic)
development of geometry. Loosely speaking, I have
assumed that the reader is familiar with the definitions
and concepts of Euclidean geometry and with the bare

essentials of trigonometry. For example, the notions of angle, parallelism, and area are assumed. It is further assumed that the reader knows the definitions of the sine, cosine, and tangent functions (in the naive sense, as ratios of the sides of a right triangle). In regard to results from geometry and trigonometry, I have indeed taken very little for granted. Samples of geometric information that are called upon are: formulas for the area of a parallelogram and volume of a parallelopiped, the fact that two points determine a unique line, and the result that opposite sides of a parallelogram are equal. In Chapter 3 I use the law of cosines for motivation, but the reader who has not seen it before will be consoled by a proof given shortly thereafter.

It is entirely possible to give a vector development of Euclidean geometry from "scratch." In fact, some people believe that a first course in geometry should begin with vectors. Others believe that the coordinate method should be given at the outset, and still others have faith in a combination of approaches. The coordinate development, in various forms, has recently been adopted by several of the current groups interested in rewriting the high school mathematics curriculum. For the reader interested in seeing how a strict vector approach would do the job, I strongly recommend the excellent paper "Geometric Vector Analysis and the Concept of Vector Space" by Professor Walter Prenowitz. This fine exposition constitutes one of the chapters of the *Twenty-Third Yearbook* of the National Council of Teachers of Mathematics.

Sincere thanks and appreciation are due to the teachers who came to Carleton in the summer of 1959 in the hope of comfortably learning mathematics in cool Minnesota but who, instead, labored and perspired under the strains of vector geometry and the 96 % humidity. For reading the manuscript and for their valuable suggestions I am especially grateful to Mr. Saul Birnbaum of the New Lincoln School in New York City, Professor Roy Dubisch of the University of Washington, Professor J. M. Sachs of the Chicago Technical College, and my Carleton colleague, Professor William B. Houston, Jr. Also, special thanks go to Professor Dick Wick Hall, who courageously used the text in mimeograph form at a National Science Foundation Institute in the summer of 1961. This experience enabled Professor Hall to contribute substantially by pointing out my errors in judgment and typography.

SEYMOUR SCHUSTER

Northfield, Minnesota
January, 1962

contents

Chapter 1   ELEMENTARY OPERATIONS   *1*

1. Introduction · 2. Definition of vector · 3.
Fundamental properties · 4. Linear combinations
of vectors · 5. Auxiliary point technique · 6.
Uniqueness of representations.

Chapter 2   VECTORS IN COORDINATE SYSTEMS   *40*

7. Rectangular systems and orientation · 8.
Basis vectors and applications · 9. The complex
plane.

Chapter 3   INNER PRODUCTS   *60*

10. Definition · 11. Properties of inner product ·
12. Components · 13. Inner product formulas ·
14. Work.

Chapter 4   ANALYTIC GEOMETRY   76

15. Our point of view · 16. The straight line · 17.
Analytic geometry of the line continued · 18.
Distance from a point to a line · 19. Analytic
method of proof · 20. Circles · 21. Spheres · 22.
Planes · 23. Determining a plane by points on it ·
24. Distance from a point to a plane · 25. The
straight line in three dimensions · 26. Angle between two lines · 27. Intersection of a line with a
plane · 28. Angle between a line and a plane.

Chapter 5   CROSS PRODUCTS   *135*

29. Cross products · 30. Triple scalar product ·
31. Distance from a point to a plane · 32. Distance between two lines · 33. Triple cross
products.

Chapter 6   TRIGONOMETRY   *151*

34. Plane trigonometry · 35. Spherical
trigonometry.

Chapter 7   MORE GEOMETRY   *160*

36. Loci defined by inequalities · 37. A few
booby traps · 38. Segments and convexity · 39.
Linear programming · 40. Theorems arising in
more general geometries · 41. Applications of
parametric equations to locus problems · 42.
Rigid motions.

APPENDIX   *204*
ANSWERS   *206*
INDEX   *211*

elementary vector geometry

1

elementary operations

1. INTRODUCTION

The history of the development of mathematical ideas indicates that abstract concepts arise generally from roots in some "practical" problem. Arithmetic stemmed from problems of counting, geometry arose from problems of surveying land in Egypt, and calculus developed principally from the efforts to solve the problems of motion. Mathematics, however, goes quite beyond the point of solving merely the problems that initiate the particular study, for mathematics is concerned with building a *deductive science* that is general and *abstract*, that may have a wide range of application. By a *deductive science* we mean, briefly, a logical development that begins with a basic framework consisting of a set of *assumptions* (called *axioms* or *postulates*) and a set of terms used in stating the assumptions. All the logical consequences of the assumptions are then the theorems of the deductive science, which is concerned with abstractions or idealizations of concepts from the original problem rather than with the original problem itself. For example, the study of geometry is based on a set of assumptions that deal essentially with lines and points rather than with fences and fenceposts. Line is an abstract concept; it is an idealization of the fence, and it admits to all sorts of other interpretations: a ray of light, the edge of a board, the path of a molecule under some circumstances, and a host of still others. Thus geometry, with its origins in surveying, finds application in a variety of problems.

The pure mathematician, however, goes on—and far beyond. Because once he begins a mathematical study, he is free to exercise his imagination by making logical deductions (proving theorems) and developing theories that are quite apart from the realities of the motivating problem. For the mathematician there is a reality within his deductive science. Again drawing from geometry for illustration, we can point to the developments of four dimensional geometry—even *n*-dimensional geometry—in spite of the fact that our physical world is three dimensional, or to the invention of non-Euclidean geometries, that contradict Euclid's Parallel Postulate (which, for over 2000 years, was accepted as absolute mathematical truth). Such creations by mathematicians were consequences of strong imagination and quite beyond the consideration of any elementary problem in the physical world.

Vector analysis is also a subject that has its roots in physical problems. It was developed primarily to handle problems in physics, initially problems in mechanics but, later, problems in various other branches of physical science. Developments of the nineteenth and twentieth centuries have resulted in the *abstract concept of a vector* and, consequently, in a wide range of interpretations of this abstract concept. The result is that vectors now play a prominent role in a variety of studies, to name just a few: physical chemistry, fluid-flow theory, electro-magnetic theory, economics, psychology, and electrocardiography.

Geometry books are always filled with illustrations in spite of the fact that point, line, and circle are abstract concepts that do not exist in physical reality and in spite of the fact that beginning students are apprised of the abstract nature of the subject at the very beginning of their course. The reason is quite simple. Abstract reasoning is difficult; students therefore need—or are at least assisted by—the help of some real *model* (or *interpretation*) of the abstract concepts. Consequently, a small dot marked with a sharp pencil is a convenient model for the concept of point, and a sharp pencil drawn along the edge of a ruler leaves a mark that is used as a model for the concept of line. Such pencil marks are a great convenience for beginners until they get to feel at home in the subject and begin to feel that there is a reality in geometry itself. Later in their mathematical studies students encounter other abstract concepts, but by this time they can, and do, use *geometric models* to assist them in still more abstract reasoning. This pattern of development is precisely what occurs in the study of vectors. Although the concept of vector can be made abstract, a geometric model (directed line segment) is the crutch that assists the beginner in developing steady legs in the field that is new to him.

It is the author's view that steady legs in abstract vector algebra are developed slowly and that reasoning in the model (now geometry) for some extended period should be done preliminary to engaging in the abstract study. Therefore this entire textbook concerns itself with a geometric study of vectors (i.e., the application of vectors to geometry), in contrast to the general abstract study of vectors. Let us begin.

2. DEFINITION OF VECTOR

Earlier we pointed out that the idea of vector came originally from physics. Therefore, let us consider— from the physicist's point of view—the statement of the television announcer who, before giving his final "Good night," states, "The temperature is now 37° and the wind is 12 miles per hour in a northeasterly direction." In this simple weather announcement we observe examples of two distinctly different types of quantities in the sense that the first (temperature) requires only a single number—with units, of course—for its description, whereas the second quantity (wind velocity) requires two facts, magnitude and direction. These examples are typical of the quantities encountered in elementary physics. Hence, the following simple classification is made: *quantities that possess only magnitude are singled out and called scalars*, whereas *quantities that possess both magnitude and direction are called vectors.*

In addition to temperature, examples of scalar quantities are mass, length, area, and volume; and, in addition to velocity, examples of vectors are force, acceleration, and electrical intensity.

Just as the mathematician desires a geometric model for his general concepts, so does the physicist. For geometry—to the trained physicist—also has a reality by means of which he can "visualize" and be aided in his reasoning. A convenient geometric model for a vector is a directed line segment ($\nearrow$) because this possesses both magnitude (length) and direction, simultaneously. This model, which suits the needs of physicists, is also quite satisfactory for our purposes, for it is our aim to study geometry (by means of vectors). Hence, for our mathematical development, we make the following formal definition.

Definition. *A vector is a directed line segment.* We shall use **boldface type** to indicate a vector. The symbol $|\mathbf{A}|$

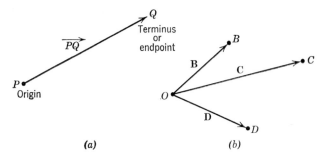

FIGURE 1

will be used to designate the length of vector **A**. In the event that the vector we speak of is the directed segment PQ, we emphasize its vector nature by writing $\overrightarrow{PQ}$, P being the *origin* and Q being the *terminus* or *endpoint* of PQ (see Figure 1a). Another useful convention when referring to several vectors $\overrightarrow{OB}$, $\overrightarrow{OC}$, and $\overrightarrow{OD}$ with a common origin O is to call these vectors **B**, **C**, and **D**, respectively. That is, if a discussion is concerned with several vectors emanating from a single point, we may designate them merely by their individual endpoints (see Figure 1b).

A vector of length one is called a *unit vector*. The notion of a vector of zero length (with any direction), although apparently peculiar, is actually a great convenience. We refer to such a vector as *the zero vector* and shall point to its usefulness from time to time. The notation for the zero vector is **O**. The direction of the zero vector is discussed further in Section 4.

Scalars, being merely magnitudes, will be real-numbered quantities. (In more advanced mathematics scalars may be elements of the complex numbers; indeed, they may be from any number field. Our needs, however, do not require such generality and will therefore be satisfied by restricting scalars to the real numbers.) They are designated by lower-case Latin letters: a, b, c, or by numerals.

3. FUNDAMENTAL PROPERTIES

Our desire is to build an algebra of vectors, and to this end we must first present a criterion for calling two vectors equal.

Definition. *Two vectors* **A** *and* **B** *are called equal (written* **A** = **B**) *if and only if*[1] *the following three conditions hold:*

(i) **A** *is parallel to* **B**;[2]

(ii) **A** *and* **B** *possess the same sense of direction; and*

(iii) $|\mathbf{A}| = |\mathbf{B}|$, *i.e., the length of* **A** *equals the length of* **B**.

It cannot be emphasized too strongly that vectors may be equal even if they do not possess the same position in space. As a matter of fact, our definition indicates that a vector **A** may be relocated provided that we move it rigidly to a position parallel to its original position and that we do not change its length or sense of direction (see Figure 2a). It may therefore be relocated in a position with its origin anywhere in space that we choose. When vectors are given this freedom, they are termed *free*.

[1] The phrase "if and only if" points up the fact that the definition is actually a double implication, or logical equivalence. That is, (a) If **A** = **B**, then conditions (i), (ii), and (iii) hold; and (b) If conditions (i), (ii), and (iii) hold, then **A** = **B**.

[2] We use the word *parallel* in the more general sense to mean "parallel or on the same line." Although this usage is not given in high school geometry, it is quite common in analytic geometry, where two lines possessing equal slopes are called parallel (see Section 16). Thus a line is parallel to itself, and *a vector is equal to itself*. The latter would not be true if we didn't use "parallel" in this generalized sense. Figure 2b exhibits two equal vectors on the same line.

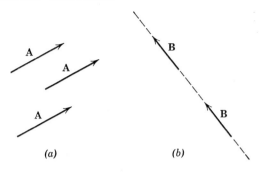

FIGURE 2

In the study of geometry this liberty to make displacements of vectors is highly advantageous. In the applications of vectors to other sciences this freedom is not always granted, for it is necessary to restrict vectors to some degree. For example, in the mechanics of rigid bodies it is often required that a vector be confined to a line; that is, it may be moved rigidly but only in the line it lay originally. This line is referred to as its *line of action*. In Figure 3*a* we show three vectors, **F**, **G**, and **H**, which represent three forces of the same magnitude, acting on parallel lines and having the same sense of

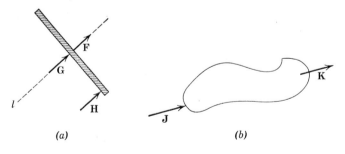

FIGURE 3

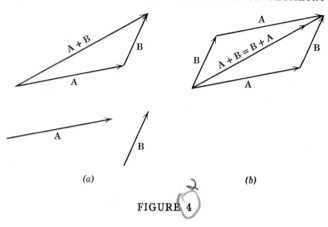

(a)   *(b)*

FIGURE 4

direction. They would therefore be equal according to our definition. **F** represents a pulling force at the center of the bar and **G** represents a pushing force at the center of the bar. **F** and **G** would have the same mechanical effect and are therefore considered mechanically equal. However, **H** applied at the end of the bar would effect a turning motion, which is quite different from the effect of **F** = **G**. Thus **H** is not equal to the other forces. In such studies it would be natural to insist that two forces having different lines of action be unequal. This justifies the stipulation in the theory of mechanics of rigid bodies, of permitting a vector to be displaced only along its line of action.

If the field of application were the theory of elasticity, then it would be necessary to restrict (force) vectors still more. Figure 3*b* shows two forces **J** and **K**, both of the same magnitude and directed along the same line of action, acting on a soft plasticlike material. **K** has the effect of stretching the mass, whereas **J** has the effect of compressing it. This illustration indicates why, in the theory of elasticity, two vectors applied at different points are not considered equal.   In this field a vector is restricted to its original position; there is no freedom to displace it.   Such vectors are called *bound*.

We state, with emphasis, once again: *all vectors in this book are free, in accordance with our definition of equality.*

Addition.   Let **A** and **B** be any two vectors (Figure 4a). We can select a location for vector **B** so that its origin is placed at the terminus of **A**.   Now we construct a third vector, called **A + B**, whose origin coincides with the origin of **A** and whose terminus coincides with the terminus of **B**.

The construction (Figure 4b) of **B + A** clearly indicates that **B + A = A + B**, for both are the same diagonal of the same parallelogram, and they possess the same sense of direction.   Hence we have the following result.

Theorem 1.   (*i*) *Addition of vectors is commutative; that is* **A + B = B + A**.

(ii) *Addition of vectors is associative; that is*

$$(A + B) + C = A + (B + C).$$

Part (ii) of the theorem is easily established by using the definition of addition.   Figure 5 illustrates the proof.

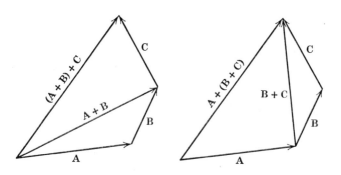

FIGURE 5

3

However, the reader is advised to phrase the proof as a logical deduction from elementary geometry independent of a figure.

EXERCISE

1. Give an elementary geometry proof of the theorem: If equal vectors are added to equal vectors, the sums are equal vectors.

As indicated in Section 1, the notion of a vector arose, historically, from an attempt to characterize physical quantities, notably force. It is interesting to note that the little-known, but nonetheless excellent, Dutch scientist, Simon Stevin (1548–1620), experimented with two forces in an effort to replace the two by a single one, called the *resultant*. He discovered that the resultant was actually the force represented by the diagonal of a parallelogram, of which the sides represented the two original forces (Figure 6). This led to his formulation of the principles of addition of forces, which he used extensively in developing a complete theory of equilibrium—the beginning of modern statics. (It is for this reason that the parallelograms of Figure 6 are sometimes referred to as parallelograms of forces.) Among the many other accomplishments of Stevin are his: (1) work on hydrostatics, which laid plans for the reclamation of the below-sea-level land of

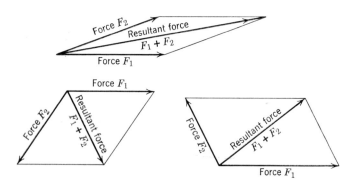

FIGURE 6

Holland, and (2) development of decimal notation for numbers with the consequent methods for computation. He was the first to give a systematic treatment of decimals. (See the chapter entitled "Stevin on Decimal Fractions" in *A Source Book in Mathematics*, by D. E. Smith, or *A History of Mathematics*, by J. F. Scott, 1960.)

Thus our definition of vector addition is consistent with the desires of the physicist who is interested in applying the techniques of vector analysis to his problems. (The student of applied science should constantly maintain a critical attitude toward the mathematical definitions, taking care to see whether or not they accurately reflect given physical situations.) Before continuing, it should be mentioned that Galileo (1564–1642), quite independently, came to the same conclusion as did Simon Stevin. Thus two scientists discovered how vectors "should" add, approximately two centuries prior to the invention of vector algebra and vector analysis in the nineteenth century.

Our definition of addition can now be extended to find the sum of n vectors: $\mathbf{A}_1 + \mathbf{A}_2 + \mathbf{A}_3 + \cdots + \mathbf{A}_n$. Of course, this can be done by grouping pairs (note part (ii) of Theorem 1) and applying the definition repeatedly. However, the geometric process might be described simply as follows: move $\mathbf{A}_2$ so that its origin is at the terminus of $\mathbf{A}_1$; move $\mathbf{A}_3$ so that its origin is at the terminus of $\mathbf{A}_2$; continue this process until $\mathbf{A}_n$ is placed with its origin at the terminus of $\mathbf{A}_{n-1}$. The sum $\mathbf{A}_1 + \mathbf{A}_2 + \mathbf{A}_3 + \cdots + \mathbf{A}_n$ is then the vector whose origin coincides with the origin of $\mathbf{A}_1$ and whose terminus coincides with the terminus of $\mathbf{A}_n$.

What would be the sum of the vectors that form a closed polygon with arrows taking us all the way around? (Try to find the answer before reading on.) Consider, for example, $\mathbf{A} + \mathbf{B} + \mathbf{C} + \mathbf{D} + \mathbf{E} + \mathbf{F}$ of Figure 7. This is the vector whose origin coincides with the origin of $\mathbf{A}$ and whose terminus coincides with the terminus of $\mathbf{F}$ after the vectors are placed "origin to terminus" as

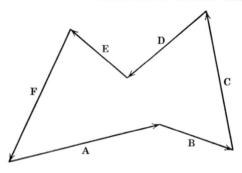

FIGURE 7

described above. Hence the origin and terminus of the sum vector are the same point, and the vector is of zero length. We then write

$$\mathbf{A} + \mathbf{B} + \mathbf{C} + \mathbf{D} + \mathbf{E} + \mathbf{F} = \mathbf{O}.$$

This argument holds for a polygon of n sides, so the answer to our query is: The zero vector.

Multiplication of a vector by a scalar. In arithmetic it is convenient to introduce multiplication as an extension of addition. For example, 3×4 may be thought of $4 + 4 + 4$. Similarly, we can—at least to begin with—

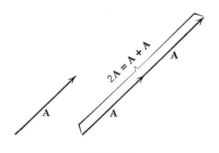

FIGURE 8

think of multiplying a vector by a scalar as an extension of vector addition. An illustration (Figure 8) might be that $2\mathbf{A}$ should represent $\mathbf{A} + \mathbf{A}$. From our definition of addition, we know vector $\mathbf{A} + \mathbf{A}$ is actually a vector parallel to $\mathbf{A}$ and having the same sense of direction as $\mathbf{A}$; however, the length of $\mathbf{A} + \mathbf{A}$ is twice the length of $\mathbf{A}$. Therefore, if $2\mathbf{A} = \mathbf{A} + \mathbf{A}$, the result of multiplying $\mathbf{A}$ by the scalar 2 is a vector parallel to $\mathbf{A}$ having the same sense of direction as $\mathbf{A}$ but with twice the length of $\mathbf{A}$.

Before proceeding to the general case of multiplying a vector by a scalar, let us consider the question of what would be appropriate for a definition of $-\mathbf{A}$. A reasonable demand might be that $\mathbf{A} + (-\mathbf{A}) = \mathbf{O}$; so let us, for the moment, stipulate this and see where it takes us. In general, if $\mathbf{A} + \mathbf{X} = \mathbf{O}$, we know that (a) $\mathbf{X}$ must be parallel to $\mathbf{A}$, (b) $|\mathbf{A}| = |\mathbf{X}|$, and (c) $\mathbf{X}$ must have a sense of direction opposite to that of $\mathbf{A}$ (Figure 9). Thus $-\mathbf{A}$ should have precisely the properties a, b, and c mentioned in the previous sentence. (Alternatively, if $\mathbf{A} + \mathbf{X} = \mathbf{O}$, then $\mathbf{A}$ followed by $\mathbf{X}$ can be thought of as a closed polygon in which the origin of $\mathbf{X}$ is at the terminus of $\mathbf{A}$.) Consequently, our definition should (and will) stipulate that multiplying by a negative scalar has the effect of changing the sense of direction of a vector. We are now ready to present a definition for the multiplication of a vector by a scalar.

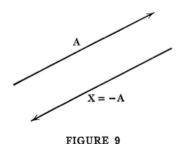

FIGURE 9

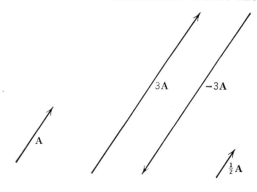

FIGURE 10

Definition.[3] *nA is a vector parallel to* **A** *with magnitude* $|n|$ *times the magnitude of* **A**. *In symbols,* $|nA| = |n|\,|A|$. *Further, if* $n > 0$, *nA is defined to have the same sense of direction as* **A**; *and if* $n < 0$, *nA is defined to have a sense of direction opposite to that of* **A**; *finally, if* $n = 0$, *nA is defined to be the zero vector (which follows from the first sentence of our definition).* Figure 10 illustrates the definition for $n = 3$, $n = -3$, and $n = \frac{1}{2}$.

Theorem 2. *If m and n are scalars, then*

$$(i) \qquad m(nA) = (mn)A.$$

$$(ii) \qquad (m + n)A = mA + nA.$$

$$(iii) \quad m(A + B) = mA + mB.$$

To illustrate, consider $m = 5$ and $n = -2$. Then $nA = -2A$, a vector twice the length of **A** but directed

---

[3] The symbol $|n|$ refers to the *absolute value* of n, which is defined as follows: If $n \geq 0$, then $|n| = n$; and if $n \leq 0$, then $|n| = -n$. The definition asserts that the absolute value of a number is always non-negative; e.g., $|3| = 3$, $|-3| = 3$, and $|0| = 0$. We shall need the fact that $|mn| = |m|\,|n|$, the truth of which should be clear from the definition.

oppositely to **A**. (i) states:

$$5(-2\mathbf{A}) = (5)(-2)\mathbf{A} = -10\mathbf{A}.$$

(ii) states: $(5 + (-2))\mathbf{A} = 5\mathbf{A} + (-2)\mathbf{A}$ or

$$3\mathbf{A} = 5\mathbf{A} + (-2)\mathbf{A}.$$

(iii) states: $5(\mathbf{A} + \mathbf{B}) = 5\mathbf{A} + 5\mathbf{B}$.

Proof. (i) By examining the length of the left member of (i), our definition of multiplication of a vector by a scalar yields

$$|m(n\mathbf{A})| = |m|\,|n\mathbf{A}| = |m|\,|n|\,|\mathbf{A}| = |mn|\,|\mathbf{A}| \\ = |(mn)\mathbf{A}|. \quad (1)$$

Equation 1 proves that the vectors of (i) are equal in length. That they are parallel follows from the fact that both are multiplies of **A**. The reader is left to check that the directions have the same sense. (*Hint.* Use the definition of $n\mathbf{A}$.)

(ii) If $m + n = 0$, both sides of (ii) represent vectors that point in the same direction as **A**. If $m + n < 0$, both sides of (ii) represent vectors that point in the direction opposite to that of **A**. The comparison of their lengths is left to the reader. (*Hint.* Use the definition of $n\mathbf{A}$.)

(iii) Let us suppose that **A** and **B** are nonparallel and nonzero. We consider the triangle PQR, which defines $\mathbf{A} + \mathbf{B}$ (see Figure 11), by having $\mathbf{A} = \overrightarrow{PQ}$, $\mathbf{B} = \overrightarrow{QR}$, then $\overrightarrow{PR} = \mathbf{A} + \mathbf{B}$. We construct triangle $P'Q'R'$, where $m\mathbf{A} = \overrightarrow{P'Q'}$, $m\mathbf{B} = \overrightarrow{Q'R'}$, then $\overrightarrow{P'R'} = m\mathbf{A} + m\mathbf{B}$. Since $m\mathbf{A}\|\mathbf{A}$ and $m\mathbf{B}\|\mathbf{B}$, triangle PQR is similar to triangle $P'Q'R'$. Thus $\overrightarrow{P'R'}$ is $m(\mathbf{A} + \mathbf{B})$, and we have the result that $m(\mathbf{A} + \mathbf{B}) = m\mathbf{A} + m\mathbf{B}$.

The reader should consider two questions concerning the proof of (iii). The first is: What of the direction of

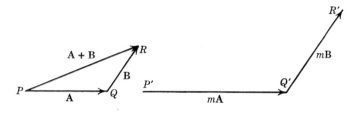

FIGURE 11

$m(\mathbf{A} + \mathbf{B})$ as compared to that of $m\mathbf{A} + m\mathbf{B}$? The proof explicitly concerned itself with the lengths and parallelism of the two vectors, but it did not discuss sense of direction. The second question is: Does the proof break down if $\mathbf{A}\|\mathbf{B}$?

NOTE. Since part (i) of Theorem 2 states that a change of parenthesis is legitimate, we now know there would be no confusion if we eliminate the parenthesis entirely and write $mn\mathbf{A}$. For example,

$$3(2\mathbf{A}) = (3 \cdot 2)\mathbf{A} = 3 \cdot 2\mathbf{A} = 6\mathbf{A}.$$

Subtraction. As in elementary arithmetic, where subtraction is an operation that is the inverse of addition, we define subtraction of vectors as the inverse of vector addition. More precisely, if α is a real number, we write $\alpha - \alpha = \alpha + (-\alpha) = 0$. This equation expresses the fact that subtraction is defined in terms of addition and that subtraction is the inverse of addition. Mathematicians say that the real number $-\alpha$ is the *inverse* of α relative to the operation of addition or simply that $-\alpha$ is the *additive inverse* of α (similarly, α is the additive inverse of $-\alpha$). We carry these ideas over to vectors in defining subtraction.

Definition. $\mathbf{A} - \mathbf{B} = \mathbf{A} + (-\mathbf{B})$ *where* $-\mathbf{B}$ *is written to mean* $-1\mathbf{B}$.

Geometrically the operation of subtraction can take any of the forms presented in Figure 12. Note that the diagonal **A** of the parallelogram is equal to the sum **B** + (**A** − **B**) and also to the sum (**A** − **B**) + **B**. Such algebraic checking is advised for the beginner who is having difficulty in finding the correct orientation for the difference vector **A** − **B**. With these few tools of addition and subtraction we can begin applying vectors to elementary geometry.

EXAMPLE 1. We shall use our vector operations to work an elementary exercise, one equivalent to the theorem which states that the diagonals of a parallelogram bisect each other. Let O, B, and C be three points not on one line. Call M the midpoint of segment BC (see Figure 13a). We shall prove that $\overrightarrow{OM} = \frac{1}{2}(\overrightarrow{OB} + \overrightarrow{OC})$. In accordance with the convention discussed on page 5, we shall write $\mathbf{B} = \overrightarrow{OB}$, $\mathbf{C} = \overrightarrow{OC}$ and $\mathbf{M} = \overrightarrow{OM}$. Then

$$\mathbf{M} = \mathbf{B} + \overrightarrow{BM}$$

and $\mathbf{M} = \mathbf{C} - \overrightarrow{MC} = \mathbf{C} - \overrightarrow{BM}$ (since $\overrightarrow{BM} = \overrightarrow{MC}$).

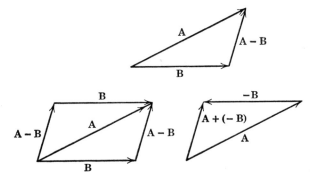

FIGURE 12

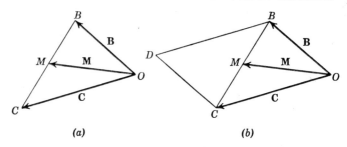

(a)   *(b)*

FIGURE 13

Adding, we get

$$2\mathbf{M} = \mathbf{B} + \mathbf{C}$$

or
$$\mathbf{M} = \tfrac{1}{2}(\mathbf{B} + \mathbf{C}).$$

If we consider our figure to be part of a parallelogram $OBDC$ (Figure 13b), then the result states that the line joining vertex O to the midpoint of diagonal BC is one half the diagonal OD, for $|\overrightarrow{OD}| = |\mathbf{B} + \mathbf{C}|$. In equivalent (and more usual) language we may conclude that the diagonals of a parallelogram bisect each other.

EXAMPLE 2. Prove that the line joining the midpoints of any two sides of a triangle is parallel to the third and equal to one half of it.

In triangle PQR (see Figure 14) let M and N be midpoints of PQ and PR, respectively. Call

$$\mathbf{A} = \overrightarrow{PN} = \overrightarrow{NR}, \ \ \mathbf{B} = \overrightarrow{PM} = \overrightarrow{MQ}, \ \ \mathbf{C} = \overrightarrow{MN}, \ \ \text{and} \ \ \mathbf{D} = \overrightarrow{QR}.$$

Then $\ \ \ \mathbf{C} = \mathbf{A} - \mathbf{B} \ \ $ and $\ \ \mathbf{C} + \mathbf{A} - \mathbf{D} - \mathbf{B} = \mathbf{O}.$

(Note that these equations follow from summing vectors about triangle MNP and quadrilateral $MNRQ$, respectively.) Adding vector $\mathbf{D}$ to both sides of the last equation, we get

$$\mathbf{C} + \mathbf{A} - \mathbf{B} = \mathbf{D}.$$

Since $\mathbf{C} = \mathbf{A} - \mathbf{B}$, we have $2\mathbf{C} = \mathbf{D}$, which (by the definition of equality of vectors) proves simultaneously that $NM \| RQ$ and that the segment NM equals one half of the base RQ.

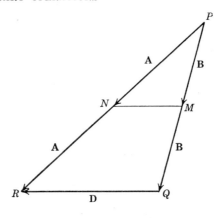

FIGURE 14

EXERCISES

1. Establish the easily remembered SHORTCUT LEMMA: $\overrightarrow{AB} + \overrightarrow{BC} = \overrightarrow{AC}$. (This lemma has also been appropriately named the Bypass Lemma by Professor D. W. Hall.)

2. Reproduce Figure 15 on another sheet. Then construct and label the vectors $\mathbf{C} - \mathbf{A}$, $\mathbf{B} - \mathbf{C}$, $\mathbf{B} + \mathbf{C}$, and $-\mathbf{B} - \mathbf{C}$.

3. Show that $\overrightarrow{PQ} + \overrightarrow{RS} = 2\overrightarrow{MN}$, where P, Q, R, and S are four arbitrarily chosen points and where M and N are the

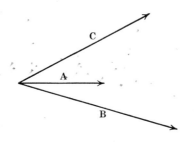

FIGURE 15

midpoints of PR and QS, respectively. (*Hint.* Sum the vectors around the polygon $NMRS$ and $NMPQ$.)

4. Draw triangle ABC, with P the midpoint of AB, Q the midpoint of BC, and R the midpoint of CA. If X is any point, show that $\overrightarrow{XA} + \overrightarrow{XB} + \overrightarrow{XC} = \overrightarrow{XP} + \overrightarrow{XQ} + \overrightarrow{XR}$.

5. A sailboat is acted upon by the wind and current. The wind velocity is 8 mph E and the current velocity is 5 mph N. Compute the magnitude of the resulting force and give a geometric construction that shows the direction of the resultant.

6. Using the fact that the sum of the forces (vectors) acting on a body in equilibrium is the zero vector, solve the following problem.

A weight of 100 lb hangs by a wire and is pushed by a horizontal force until the wire makes an angle of $\pi/4$ (or $45°$) with the vertical. Find the magnitude of the horizontal force and the tension in the wire.

7. Show that the midpoints of consecutive sides of a quadrilateral are vertices of a parallelogram.

8. If A, B, C, and D are any four points (not necessarily in a plane), prove that $\overrightarrow{AB} + \overrightarrow{AD} + \overrightarrow{CB} + \overrightarrow{CD} = 4\overrightarrow{PQ}$ where P and Q are the midpoints of AC and BD. (How does this relate to Exercise 2?)

9. Using the definition of subtraction, the commutative and associative properties of addition, show that the sums $\mathbf{B} + (\mathbf{A} - \mathbf{B})$ and $(\mathbf{A} - \mathbf{B}) + \mathbf{B}$, do actually reduce to equal $\mathbf{A}$.

10. Establish the uniqueness of $\mathbf{O}$, thus justifying the terminology: *the* zero vector. (*Hint.* Consider the possibility of a vector $\mathbf{O'}$ that has the properties of $\mathbf{O}$. Then prove that $\mathbf{O'} = \mathbf{O}$.)

4. LINEAR COMBINATIONS OF VECTORS

Now that we have learned to add and subtract vectors, and also to multiply vectors by scalars, we can combine these operations to generate new vectors and to enrich our algebra of vectors. For example, if we are given $\mathbf{A}$

and $\mathbf{B}$, we can perform our various operations to get $\mathbf{A} + \mathbf{B}$, $\mathbf{A} - \mathbf{B}$, $2\mathbf{A} - 3\mathbf{B}$, $5\mathbf{A} + 6\mathbf{B}$, etc. Such combinations of $\mathbf{A}$ and $\mathbf{B}$ are called *linear combinations* of $\mathbf{A}$ and $\mathbf{B}$. The set of all linear combinations of $\mathbf{A}$ and $\mathbf{B}$ could be written $\{x\mathbf{A} + y\mathbf{B} \mid x \text{ and } y \text{ real}\}$.[4] The definition of linear combinations is now extended in the following way: If $\mathbf{A}_1$, $\mathbf{A}_2$, $\mathbf{A}_3$, . . . , $\mathbf{A}_n$ are n vectors and x_1, x_2, x_3, . . . , x_n are n scalars, the vector

$$x_1\mathbf{A}_1 + x_2\mathbf{A}_2 + x_3\mathbf{A}_3 + \cdots + x_n\mathbf{A}_n$$

is said to be a *linear combination* of $\mathbf{A}_1$, $\mathbf{A}_2$, $\mathbf{A}_3$, . . . , $\mathbf{A}_n$.

The present section is devoted to the study of linear combinations of certain sets of vectors, and the ideas contained herein are perhaps the most difficult in the entire book. Thus we shall proceed slowly. The reader is cautioned to study the definitions and to *take them literally!*

We noted earlier that the equation $\mathbf{A} + \mathbf{X} = \mathbf{O}$ implies that $\mathbf{X} = -\mathbf{A}$, that is, $\mathbf{X}$ is the vector obtained by multiplying $\mathbf{A}$ by -1. Since $\mathbf{X}$ can be derived from $\mathbf{A}$, we could, in a sense, say that $\mathbf{X}$ is dependent upon $\mathbf{A}$; or, conversely, that $\mathbf{A}$ is dependent upon $\mathbf{X}$. Similarly, if we began with $\mathbf{A} + 3\mathbf{Y} = \mathbf{O}$, we could write

$$\mathbf{Y} = -\tfrac{1}{3}\mathbf{A}$$

and
$$\mathbf{A} = -3\mathbf{Y}.$$

Thus $\mathbf{Y}$ is shown to depend on $\mathbf{A}$ and $\mathbf{A}$ to depend on $\mathbf{Y}$. It might be preferable to state simply that $\mathbf{A}$ and $\mathbf{Y}$ are dependent. It is almost trivial to observe that such dependency would be impossible to show if the scalar coefficients of $\mathbf{A}$ and $\mathbf{Y}$ were both zero. Hence we exclude this case from consideration in making the following definition.

---

[4] The symbolism $\{\mid\}$, borrowed from set theory, is useful in defining sets in the following way: $\{z \mid S(z)\}$ represents the *set of all z satisfying the condition or sentence $S(z)$.*

Definition. *Two vectors* **A** *and* **B** *are called* linearly dependent *if and only if there exists two scalars a and b, not both zero, so that* $a\mathbf{A} + b\mathbf{B} = \mathbf{O}$.

Remark: The student should recognize the fact that definitions of words are statements of logical equivalence (see footnote 1, page 6); i.e., both the statement and its converse hold. Using our present definition to illustrate this explicitly, we would say that the definition states: (1) **A** and **B** being linearly dependent implies that there exist scalars a and b, *not both of them zero*, so that $a\mathbf{A} + b\mathbf{B} = \mathbf{O}$; and (2) if a relation $a\mathbf{A} + b\mathbf{B} = \mathbf{O}$ holds, with *not both a and b equal to zero* (i.e., at least one being nonzero), then **A** and **B** are linearly dependent.

Algebraically our definition is equivalent to saying that two vectors are linearly dependent if and only if (see footnote 1 for explanation of the phrase "if and only if") one of them is a scalar multiple of the other (show this!). A geometric interpretation would be the following: Two vectors are linearly dependent if and only if they are parallel. The reader can verify these interpretations formally by constructing a general argument of the form that preceded our definition. One fine point, however, must be mentioned; this concerns the presence of **O** as one of the vectors under consideration. First, we note that **O** and any vector **A** are linearly dependent, for $1\mathbf{O} + 0\mathbf{A} = \mathbf{O}$, which is the defining condition for **O** and **A** to be linearly dependent (1 is the required nonzero scalar). Our geometric interpretation would say that **O** is parallel to **A**, where **A** may be any vector. This may appear strange to the beginning student of vectors; however, it is a matter of great convenience to retain the convention that the *zero vector is parallel to every vector!* Instead of regarding the zero vector as having no direction (as would appeal to some), we regard **O** as having any direction. Vectors specify magnitude *and* direction, so we choose to say that **O** has any or all directions simultaneously. Of course, the zero vector is the only vector with such a property, for any other vector (line segment of nonzero length) has a unique direction. Later, when we work with perpendicular vectors, we shall have occasion to regard the zero vector as perpendicular to every vector. Again, this is consistent with the idea that the zero vector has any direction.

In the event that two vectors are not linearly dependent, we call them *linearly independent*. Summarizing, we say that:

(1) A pair of vectors, of which one is a zero vector, is a linearly dependent set of vectors.

(2) A pair of parallel nonzero vectors is a linearly dependent set.

(3) A pair of nonzero, nonparallel vectors is a linearly independent set.

Confining our attention merely to pairs of vectors would contradict the generalizing spirit of mathematics and, furthermore, would leave us with a rather meager theory of linear dependence. We therefore proceed to extend our notions with the following definition.

Definition. *A set* $\mathbf{A}_1$, $\mathbf{A}_2$, . . . , $\mathbf{A}_n$ *of n vectors is called linearly dependent if there exist a set of scalars* $x_1, x_2, \ldots, x_n$, *so that*

$$x_1\mathbf{A}_1 + x_2\mathbf{A}_2 + \cdots + x_n\mathbf{A}_n = \mathbf{O},$$

where not all the x's are zero (i.e. when at least one does not equal zero). If, on the other hand, the equation

$$x_1\mathbf{A}_1 + x_2\mathbf{A}_2 + \cdots + x_n\mathbf{A}_n = \mathbf{O}$$

implies that $x_1 = x_2 = \cdots = x_n = 0$, *then the set* $\mathbf{A}_1$, $\mathbf{A}_2$, . . . , $\mathbf{A}_n$ *is said to be linearly independent.* For example, if three vectors, $\overrightarrow{AB}$, $\overrightarrow{CD}$, and $\overrightarrow{EF}$, are given, one of the following cases must occur: (a) It is possible to find three scalars a, b, and c, not all zero, such that

$$a\overrightarrow{AB} + b\overrightarrow{CD} + c\overrightarrow{EF} = \mathbf{O}. \qquad (*)$$

(b) It is not possible to find three such scalars. In case (a) the three vectors are said to be linearly dependent. In case (b) they are said to be linearly independent. In both cases (*) will hold if $a = 0$, $b = 0$, and $c = 0$.

The jump from two vectors to n vectors may be rather steep, so we shall provide an intermediate step in the form of a geometric theorem.

Theorem 3. *If **A** and **B** are linearly independent, then any third vector **C**, which is parallel to (or in) the plane determined by **A** and **B**, can be expressed as a linear combination of **A** and **B**.*

Proof. It should be recalled that vectors may be arranged so that they possess a common origin, that is, we are dealing with *free* vectors. Therefore, even when the segments representing **A**, **B**, and **C** might be in space, they can be moved to positions in the same plane (see Figure 16). For **A** and **B** with a common origin determine a plane; and **C** (being parallel to this plane) may then be displaced so that it is actually in the plane of **A** and **B**.

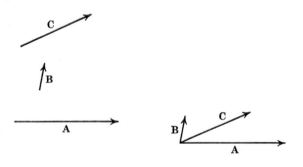

FIGURE 16

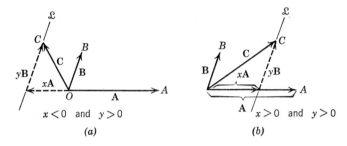

FIGURE 17

Now, if **C** is a nonzero vector, there is a parallelogram with diagonal **C** and with edges along **A** and **B**. An explicit construction of this parallelogram is given in Figure 17 and can be described as follows: Call O the common origin of the vectors **A**, **B**, and **C**, and call A, B, and C the respective endpoints of the three vectors. Construct a line $\mathcal{L}$ through C parallel to **B**, and call D the intersection of $\mathcal{L}$ with the line of action of **A** (when the origin of **A** is O). Then $\overrightarrow{OD}$, being parallel to **A**, is some multiple of **A**; let us say $\overrightarrow{OD} = x\mathbf{A}$. Furthermore, $\overrightarrow{DC}$, being parallel to **B**, is some multiple of **B**; let us say $\overrightarrow{DC} = y\mathbf{B}$. Then

$$\mathbf{C} = x\mathbf{A} + y\mathbf{B}, \tag{2}$$

which shows **C** to be a linear combination of **A** and **B**.

In the event that **C** is the zero vector, the theorem is trivially true, for

$$\mathbf{O} = 0\mathbf{A} + 0\mathbf{B}, \tag{3}$$

and our proof is complete.

To associate more strongly the idea of Theorem 3 with the concept of linear dependence, we state the

Corollary. *Any three vectors in the same plane are linearly dependent.*

Proof. Equations 2 and 3 imply that there exist scalars x_1, x_2, x_3, (not all zero), so that

$$x_1\mathbf{A} + x_2\mathbf{B} + x_3\mathbf{C} = \mathbf{O}.$$

For, when $\mathbf{C} \neq \mathbf{O}$, at least one of x and y in (2) is non-zero. When $\mathbf{C} = \mathbf{O}$, we can set x_3 equal to any real number, say $x_3 = 1$, and $x_1 = x_2 = 0$.

EXAMPLE 3. We shall use the concept of linear combination to achieve another view of Example 1. Suppose we wish to prove that the diagonals of a parallelogram bisect each other. Let the parallelogram be $OABC$ (see Figure 18), with P the intersection of the diagonals. Again, using the convention of writing $\mathbf{P} = \overrightarrow{OP}$, $\mathbf{A} = \overrightarrow{OA}$, and $\mathbf{B} = \overrightarrow{OB}$, we have $\mathbf{P} = m\mathbf{B}$ $= m(\mathbf{A} + \mathbf{C})$ and $\overrightarrow{PA} = n(\mathbf{A} - \mathbf{C})$, where m and n are scalars to be determined. Since $\mathbf{A} = \mathbf{P} + \overrightarrow{PA}$, we may write

$$\mathbf{A} = m(\mathbf{A} + \mathbf{C}) + n(\mathbf{A} - \mathbf{C}),$$

and grouping the $\mathbf{A}$-terms and $\mathbf{C}$-terms gives

$$(m + n - 1)\mathbf{A} + (m - n)\mathbf{C} = \mathbf{O}.$$

Because $\mathbf{A}$ and $\mathbf{C}$ are linearly independent, their scalar coefficients in the last equation must both be zero. Hence

$$m + n = 1 \quad \text{and} \quad m - n = 0.$$

Thus $m = n = \frac{1}{2}$, which proves that P bisects both diagonals simultaneously.

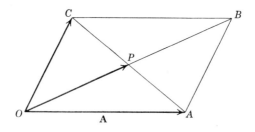

FIGURE 18

Continuing with the development on linear combinations of vectors in the plane, we next establish an important theorem that serves as a very strong instrument for work with geometric problems.

Theorem 4. *Let* **A**, **B** *and* **C** *be located so that they have a common origin O. Then:*

(i) If **C** has its endpoint on the line joining the endpoints of **A** and **B**,

$$\mathbf{C} = l\mathbf{A} + m\mathbf{B}, \quad \text{where } l + m = 1.$$

(ii) Conversely, if **C** has a representation in the form

$$\mathbf{C} = l\mathbf{A} + m\mathbf{B}, \quad \text{where } l + m = 1,$$

C has its endpoint on the line joining the endpoints of **A** and **B**.

Before proceeding with the proof, the reader should observe that the theorem is concerned with three vectors in the same plane (often called *coplanar vectors*), and if **A** and **B** are nonzero and nonparallel, then every vector in the plane of **A** and **B** (**C** being one such) is a linear combination of **A** and **B**, by Theorem 3. However, the theorem singles out particular linear combinations by means of a condition on the scalar coefficients.

For the converse point of view, we would state (and the reader should verify) that any linear combination of two linearly independent vectors, **A** and **B**, is equal to a vector in the plane of **A** and **B** when the two are situated to possess a common origin. Once again, the theorem states that certain of these linear combinations have interesting geometric implications.

Proof: (i) Here we have as our hypothesis the fact that **A**, **B**, and **C** all emanate from the same point *O*, and that **C** has its endpoint on the line joining the endpoints of **A** and **B**. We follow the convention of calling

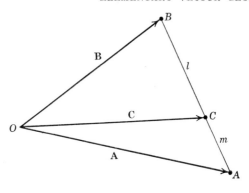

FIGURE 19

A, B, and C the endpoints of **A**, **B**, and **C**, respectively (see Figure 19).

Let C divide segment BA in the ratio $l:m$, where $l + m = 1$. (The reader should convince himself that a given ratio can always be transformed algebraically so that the two parts sum to unity.) Then

$$\mathbf{C} = \mathbf{B} + \overrightarrow{BC} = \mathbf{B} + l\overrightarrow{BA} = \mathbf{B} + l(\mathbf{A} - \mathbf{B})$$

$$= l\mathbf{A} + (1 - l)\mathbf{B}.$$

Thus $\mathbf{C} = l\mathbf{A} + m\mathbf{B}$.

(ii) For the converse, our hypothesis states that **A**, **B**, and **C** emanate from the same point and $\mathbf{C} = l\mathbf{A} + m\mathbf{B}$, where $l + m = 1$. We must show that **C** has its endpoint on the line joining the endpoints of **A** and **B**.

Now $\mathbf{C} = l\mathbf{A} + m\mathbf{B} = l\mathbf{A} + (1 - l)\mathbf{B}$;

or $\mathbf{C} = \mathbf{B} + l(\mathbf{A} - \mathbf{B})$.

A geometric examination of this last equation completes the proof, for the equation states that C may be reached by traveling from O to B, and then along line BA.

EXERCISES

1. What happens if **A** or **B** is the zero vector?

2. What are l and m if **C** = **A**?

3. What can be stated regarding the location of C if
   (a) both l and m are positive?
   (b) l is negative?
   (c) $l = 0$?

4. Give constructions for cases where
   (a) $l = m = \frac{1}{2}$;
   (b) $l = \frac{1}{3}$ and $m = \frac{2}{3}$;
   (c) $l = \frac{3}{2}$ and $m = -\frac{1}{2}$.

5. (a) If the ratio of division is $2:3 = l:m$,
       find l and m so that $l + m = 1$.
   (b) Do the same for the ratio $4:3$.
   (c) Do the same for the ratio $5:-3$.

EXAMPLE 4. Theorem 4 reduces Example 1 (p. 17) to a triviality. For, let O, B, and C be three points not on one line, with M the midpoint of BC (see Figure 20). Then M divides BC in the ratio $1:1 (= \frac{1}{2}:\frac{1}{2})$, and Theorem 4 allows us to write

$$\mathbf{M} = \tfrac{1}{2}\mathbf{B} + \tfrac{1}{2}\mathbf{C}.$$

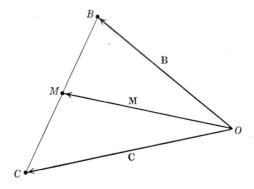

FIGURE 20

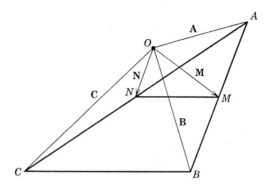

FIGURE 21

5. AUXILIARY POINT TECHNIQUE

The introduction of an auxiliary point to play the role of common origin for several vectors under consideration often facilitates the use of Theorem 4. The following three examples are devoted to an exploration of this technique.

EXAMPLE 5. We shall now provide a new approach to the problem of Example 2. Although more difficult perhaps, the new approach may be instructive.

Let triangle ABC be given, with M and N midpoints of sides AB and AC, respectively. Let O be a point in general position (not coinciding with any of the already named points or lines). Applying Theorem 4 to the three vectors $\mathbf{A}$, $\mathbf{C}$, and $\mathbf{N}$ that emanate from O (see Figure 21), we get

$$\mathbf{N} = \tfrac{1}{2}\mathbf{A} + \tfrac{1}{2}\mathbf{C};$$

and similarly,

$$\mathbf{M} = \tfrac{1}{2}\mathbf{A} + \tfrac{1}{2}\mathbf{B}.$$

Since we desire to compare MN with BC, we must examine vector $\mathbf{N} - \mathbf{M}$. Thus

$$\mathbf{N} - \mathbf{M} = \tfrac{1}{2}\mathbf{C} - \tfrac{1}{2}\mathbf{B} = \tfrac{1}{2}(\mathbf{C} - \mathbf{B}),$$

which proves both desired results: that $\mathbf{N} - \mathbf{M} \ (= \overrightarrow{MN})$ is parallel to $\mathbf{C} - \mathbf{B} \ (= \overrightarrow{BC})$ and that $\overrightarrow{MN} = \tfrac{1}{2}\overrightarrow{BC}$.

EXAMPLE 6. We shall once again prove that the diagonals of a parallelogram bisect each other, but this time by using the auxiliary point technique, Theorem 4, and still another tool that has heretofore been unemployed.

Let the parallelogram be $ABCD$, calling P the intersection of the diagonals. Furthermore, let O be a point in general position (see Figure 22). Once again, according to our convention, we write

$$\mathbf{A} = \overrightarrow{OA}, \quad \mathbf{B} = \overrightarrow{OB}, \quad \mathbf{C} = \overrightarrow{OC}, \quad \mathbf{D} = \overrightarrow{OD}, \quad \text{and } \mathbf{P} = \overrightarrow{OP}.$$

Establishing our hypothesis in vector language, we write $\overrightarrow{AD} = \overrightarrow{BC}$ or

$$\mathbf{D} - \mathbf{A} = \mathbf{C} - \mathbf{B}. \tag{4}$$

Before proceeding further, let us pause to discuss the approach. We are interested in finding the precise ratio in which P divides AC and also the ratio in which P divides BD. Thus, if we can get a representation of $\mathbf{P}$, say

$$\mathbf{P} = n\mathbf{A} + m\mathbf{C}, \quad \text{where } n + m = 1,$$

then we would know, by Theorem 4, that

$$|\overrightarrow{PC}| : |\overrightarrow{AP}| = n : m.$$

(Note how the coefficients in the statement of Theorem 4 are related to the vectors in Figure 19.) Consequently, we seek $\mathbf{P}$ as a linear combination of $\mathbf{A}$ and $\mathbf{C}$ so that the sum of the

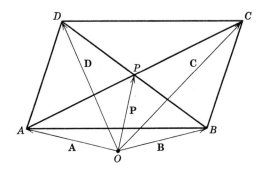

FIGURE 22

coefficients be unity.   A further observation, which is the basis
for the new tool we promised, is that **P** has two possible representations as a linear combination of two vectors emanating
from O; namely, there must be n, m, r, and s so that

$$\mathbf{P} = n\mathbf{A} + m\mathbf{C} = r\mathbf{B} + s\mathbf{D}, \tag{5}$$

where $n + m = 1$ and $r + s = 1$.

If we can succeed in producing these relations so that n, m, r,
and s are determined, we will have achieved our end.

Our first step toward (5) is to add $\mathbf{A} + \mathbf{B}$ to both members
of (4), getting

$$\mathbf{B} + \mathbf{D} = \mathbf{A} + \mathbf{C}. \tag{6}$$

Since the sum of coefficients on each side of equation (6) is 2,
we divide both members by 2, obtaining

$$\tfrac{1}{2}\mathbf{B} + \tfrac{1}{2}\mathbf{D} = \tfrac{1}{2}\mathbf{A} + \tfrac{1}{2}\mathbf{C}. \tag{7}$$

Both members of (7) comply with the conditions of Theorem
4.   Thus the left member represents a vector emanating from
O, and whose endpoint must be on BD; and the right member
represents a vector emanating from O, and whose endpoint
is on AC.   Therefore the vector (on each side) must be $\overrightarrow{OP}$,
for P is the only point on both BD and AC.   Applying Theorem
4 once again, we conclude that P divides both BD and AC in
the ratio $\tfrac{1}{2} : \tfrac{1}{2}$, which is the desired result.

EXAMPLE 7.   Employing the same techniques, we attempt
to prove the familiar result: The medians of a triangle meet in
a point two-thirds the way from a vertex to the opposite side.

Let triangle ABC have M and N midpoints of sides BC and
AC, respectively (see Figure 23).   Call P the intersection of
medians AM and BN, and let O be a point in general position.
Applying Theorem 4 to the fact that M is the midpoint of BC,
we have

$$\overrightarrow{OM} = \mathbf{M} = \tfrac{1}{2}\mathbf{B} + \tfrac{1}{2}\mathbf{C}. \tag{8}$$

Similarly, N being the midpoint of AC yields

$$\overrightarrow{ON} = \mathbf{N} = \tfrac{1}{2}\mathbf{A} + \tfrac{1}{2}\mathbf{C}. \tag{9}$$

Attempting to achieve **P** as a linear combination of **A** and **M**,
and also as a linear combination of **B** and **N**, we subtract (9)

from (8) to eliminate **C**:

$$\mathbf{M} - \mathbf{N} = \tfrac{1}{2}\mathbf{B} - \tfrac{1}{2}\mathbf{A}.$$

Then, adding $\tfrac{1}{2}\mathbf{A} + \mathbf{N}$ to both members, we get

$$\tfrac{1}{2}\mathbf{A} + \mathbf{M} = \tfrac{1}{2}\mathbf{B} + \mathbf{N}. \tag{10}$$

The sum of the coefficients on each side of (10) is $\tfrac{3}{2}$, so we multiply both members by $\tfrac{2}{3}$. Thus

$$\tfrac{1}{3}\mathbf{A} + \tfrac{2}{3}\mathbf{M} = \tfrac{1}{3}\mathbf{B} + \tfrac{2}{3}\mathbf{N}. \tag{11}$$

The left member of (11) represents a vector whose origin is O and whose endpoint is on AM, and the right member of (11) represents a vector whose origin is O and whose endpoint is on BN. But the left and right members of (11) are different representations of the same vector. This forces us to conclude that this vector is **P**, that is,

$$\mathbf{P} = \tfrac{1}{3}\mathbf{A} + \tfrac{2}{3}\mathbf{M} = \tfrac{1}{3}\mathbf{B} + \tfrac{2}{3}\mathbf{N}. \tag{12}$$

Equation 12 tells us that P divides AM in the ratio $\tfrac{2}{3} : \tfrac{1}{3}$. (Notice once again how the coefficients in the equation allow us to deduce that $|\overrightarrow{AP}| : |\overrightarrow{PM}| = |\overrightarrow{BP}| : |\overrightarrow{PN}| = \tfrac{2}{3} : \tfrac{1}{3}$.

Query: Why is it now clear that all three medians intersect in a point?

Remark. In the examples presented, the point O of common origin of the vectors was always selected in

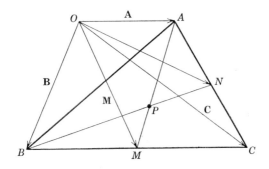

FIGURE 23

general position. This is, of course, not necessary. Moreover, placing the point of common origin in some special, judiciously chosen position often leads to considerable simplification. Exercises 1, 2, and 3, which follow, have been provided to illustrate this point.

EXERCISES

1. Carry out Example 5 when point A is the point of emanation of the several vectors in the proof.

2. Do the same for Example 6.

3. Do the same for Example 7.

4. Prove that the midpoints of consecutive sides of a quadrilateral are vertices of a parallelogram by making use of Theorem 4 (compare with Exercise 7 on p. 20).

5. Given triangle ABC with N on AB and M on AC, such that MN is parallel to BC, prove that $AN:NB = AM:MC$. What is the relationship between the fractions AN/NB and NM/BC?

6. Prove that the line joining a vertex of a parallelogram to the midpoint of an opposite side trisects the diagonal crossed by it.

7. Generalization of 6. Let $ABCD$ be a parallelogram with P on AD such that $AP = (1/n)AD$. Prove that BP intersects diagonal AC in a point Q, whose distance from A is $[1/(n + 1)]AC$.

8. (a) Prove the analogue of Theorem 3, namely: If **A**, **B**, and **C** are three nonzero, noncoplanar (cannot be placed in one plane) vectors, any vector in space can be expressed as a linear combination of **A**, **B**, and **C**. (*Hint.* A parallelepiped is the space analogue of the parallelogram in Theorem 3.)

(b) Using the result of part a, prove that any four vectors in space form a linearly dependent set.

6. UNIQUENESS OF REPRESENTATIONS

The importance of Theorem 3 lies in the statement that any vector in a plane can be expressed as a linear combination of two given linearly independent vectors in that plane.   The question we now pose is: Is such a representation unique?   More precisely, let **A** and **B** be the given linearly independent vectors and **C** some arbitrarily chosen vector in the plane of **A** and **B**.   Then, by Theorem 3, we know that there exist scalars m and n so that

$$\mathbf{C} = m\mathbf{A} + n\mathbf{B}. \tag{13}$$

But is it possible that there is another representation, perhaps different from (13), of **C** as a linear combination of **A** and **B**?

Suppose, then, that there are scalars r and s so that

$$\mathbf{C} = r\mathbf{A} + s\mathbf{B}. \tag{14}$$

Then $\qquad\qquad m\mathbf{A} + n\mathbf{B} = r\mathbf{A} + s\mathbf{B}$

and $\qquad\qquad (m - r)\mathbf{A} + (n - s)\mathbf{B} = \mathbf{O}.$

However, **A** and **B** being linearly independent implies that $m - r = 0$ and $n - s = 0$; hence, $m = r$ and $n = s$. Thus (14) is precisely the same representation of **C** as is (13).   As a result, we say that *the representation of* **C** *as a linear combination of* **A** *and* **B** *is unique.*

Similarly, we could prove the general statement that the representation of a vector as a linear combination of linearly independent vectors is unique.   Suppose

$$\mathbf{C} = a_1\mathbf{A}_1 + a_2\mathbf{A}_2 + \cdots + a_n\mathbf{A}_n = b_1\mathbf{A}_1 + b_2\mathbf{A}_2 \\ + \cdots + b_n\mathbf{A}_n,$$

where $\{\mathbf{A}_1, \mathbf{A}_2, \ldots, \mathbf{A}_n\}$[5] is a linearly independent set of vectors.   Then

$$(a_1 - b_1)\mathbf{A}_1 + (a_2 - b_2)\mathbf{A}_2 + \cdots + (a_n - b_n)\mathbf{A}_n = \mathbf{O}.$$

Again, the linear independence of the **A**'s implies that $a_1 = b_1$, $a_2 = b_2$, $\ldots$, and $a_n = b_n$. The reader

[5]Again, the brace symbolism represents a *set*, with a listing or roster of the elements of the set.

should check the geometric construction in Theorem 3 to observe the uniqueness of the representation of **C** as a linear combination of **A** and **B**.

We now employ these facts to attack some problems of geometry.

EXAMPLE 8. We return once more to the parallelogram problem in order to prove that the diagonals bisect each other. Referring to Figure 24, we write

$$\overrightarrow{PT} = m(\mathbf{A} + \mathbf{B}). \tag{15}$$

We can achieve another representation of $\overrightarrow{PT}$ by considering it as one side of triangle PQT, that is, $\overrightarrow{PT} = \overrightarrow{PQ} + \overrightarrow{QT}$. But since $\overrightarrow{QT}$ is part of diagonal $\overrightarrow{QS}$, we may write $\overrightarrow{QT} = n\overrightarrow{QS} = n(\mathbf{B} - \mathbf{A})$. Thus

$$\overrightarrow{PT} = \mathbf{A} + n(\mathbf{B} - \mathbf{A}). \tag{16}$$

From (15) and (16) we conclude that

$$\overrightarrow{PT} = m\mathbf{A} + m\mathbf{B} = (1 - n)\mathbf{A} + n\mathbf{B}.$$

Since **A** and **B** are linearly independent, the representation of $\overrightarrow{PT}$ as a linear combination of **A** and **B** must be unique. That

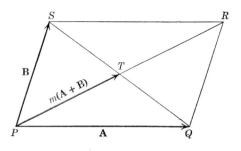

FIGURE 24

is,

$$m = 1 - n \quad \text{and} \quad m = n,$$

which imply that $m = n = \frac{1}{2}$, proving the desired result.

The reader should compare this approach with that of Example 3 to see how closely allied they are (as are the concepts of linear independence and uniqueness of representation).

EXAMPLE 9. We turn to the median problem, using the new approach. Referring to Figure 23 again, we note that $\overrightarrow{AP}$ is a part of median $\overrightarrow{AM}$, so we write $\overrightarrow{AP} = m\overrightarrow{AM}$. Similarly, $\overrightarrow{PN} = n\overrightarrow{BN}$. We seek to determine m and n.

$$\overrightarrow{AP} = m\overrightarrow{AM} = m(\tfrac{1}{2}\overrightarrow{AB} + \tfrac{1}{2}\overrightarrow{AC}). \tag{17}$$

$\overrightarrow{AB}$ and $\overrightarrow{AC}$ constitute a pair of linearly independent vectors. If we succeed in finding another representation of $\overrightarrow{AP}$ as a linear combination of $\overrightarrow{AB}$ and $\overrightarrow{AC}$, we may then employ our new technique. To this end we write

$$\overrightarrow{AP} = \overrightarrow{AN} + \overrightarrow{NP}$$

$$= \tfrac{1}{2}\overrightarrow{AC} - n\overrightarrow{BN}$$

$$= \tfrac{1}{2}\overrightarrow{AC} - n(\tfrac{1}{2}\overrightarrow{BA} + \tfrac{1}{2}\overrightarrow{BC})$$

$$= \tfrac{1}{2}\overrightarrow{AC} - \frac{n}{2}\overrightarrow{BA} - \frac{n}{2}(\overrightarrow{AC} - \overrightarrow{AB}).$$

Finally,

$$\overrightarrow{AP} = \frac{1 - n}{2}\overrightarrow{AC} + n\overrightarrow{AB}. \tag{18}$$

Comparing (17) with (18) gives

$$\frac{m}{2}\overrightarrow{AB} + \frac{m}{2}\overrightarrow{AC} = n\overrightarrow{AB} + \frac{1 - n}{2}\overrightarrow{AC},$$

which—because of the uniqueness of representation—allows

us to state that

$$\frac{m}{2} = n \qquad \text{and} \qquad \frac{m}{2} = \frac{1-n}{2}.$$

The solution to this pair of linear equations is

$$m = \frac{2}{3} \qquad \text{and} \qquad n = \frac{1}{3}.$$

The reader should observe that there was a persistent effort to get two representations of $\overrightarrow{AP}$ as *a linear combination of the two specific vectors* $\overrightarrow{AB}$ *and* $\overrightarrow{AC}$. A usual difficulty encountered by the beginning student revolves around the problem of getting the "right" relationships. He knows that he will often get two independent relationships by summing vectors around two different polygons, e.g.,

$$\overrightarrow{AP} = \overrightarrow{AB} + \overrightarrow{BP} \qquad \text{and} \qquad \overrightarrow{AP} = \overrightarrow{AN} + \overrightarrow{NP}.$$

But where to go from here? If he bears in mind the general aim to get different representations of $\overrightarrow{AP}$ (for instance) as a linear combination of the *same set of linearly independent vectors*, he may employ the technique of equating coefficients.

EXERCISES

1. Prove that the medians of a triangle meet in a point by the method of Example 9, but now by getting different representations of $\overrightarrow{NP}$.

2. Re-do Exercises 6 and 7 on page 34, making use of the method of Example 9.

3. Show that the line joining the midpoints of a median to a vertex of a triangle trisects the side opposite the vertex.

4. Given quadrilateral $ABCD$, with the condition that BD bisects AC, call F the intersection of AB and CD; call G the intersection of AD and BC. Prove that AC is parallel to FG.

(This is a difficult problem, so we provide the following hint. Let $\overrightarrow{DG} = x\overrightarrow{DA}$ and $\overrightarrow{DF} = y\overrightarrow{DC}$. Note that $\overrightarrow{DB} = u\overrightarrow{DA} + u\overrightarrow{DC}$. Then call $\overrightarrow{CG} = m\overrightarrow{BG}$ and express $\overrightarrow{BG}$ as a linear combination of $\overrightarrow{DA}$ and $\overrightarrow{DC}$, in two different ways, to determine x in terms of u. Follow a similar procedure to determine y in terms of u. Finally, if you express $\overrightarrow{GF}$ as a linear combination of $\overrightarrow{DA}$ and $\overrightarrow{DC}$, you will have the desired result.)

5. Prove the following Theorem: Let the points B' and A' divide the sides CA and CB of triangle ABC in the ratios $n:(1-n)$ and $m:(1-m)$. Let the point P be chosen so that $A'CB'P$ is a parallelogram with AC' and CB' as two of its sides. Call D the intersection of CP and AB. Then D divides AB in the ratio $m:n$. (How would you choose n and m to be sure that CD would bisect angle C?)

2

vectors in
coordinate
systems

7. RECTANGULAR SYSTEMS AND ORIENTATION

The reader is undoubtedly familiar with rectangular coordinate systems in the plane, where two perpendicular lines are chosen as axes. One is called the *x-axis*, the other the *y-axis*, and their point of intersection the *origin*. A positive direction is chosen arbitrarily on each axis, and the customary correspondence is made between points of each axis and the real numbers, where the positive real numbers are on that side of the origin arbitrarily designated as the positive part of the axis (see Figure 25). The standard convention (by no means binding) is to have the horizontal axis called the *x*-axis, with its positive side to the right of the origin O. The vertical axis is then the *y*-axis, with its positive side above the origin (see Figure 25*b*). Now, consider any point P in the plane. From P we drop perpendiculars to the axes. Call P_x and P_y the feet of these per-

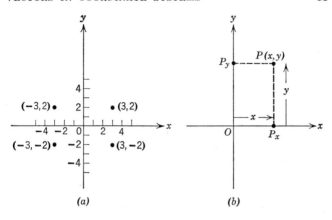

FIGURE 25

pendiculars on the x- and y-axes, respectively. The real number associated with P_x on the x-axis is called the *x-coordinate* (or *abscissa*) of P and the real number associated with P_y on the y-axis is called the *y-coordinate* (or *ordinate*) of P. P is then designated by an ordered pair (x, y) of real numbers: the abscissa occupying the first position in the pair and the ordinate occupying the second position. If the point P is on the x-axis, we give it a y-coordinate of 0; and if P is on the y-axis, we give it an x-coordinate of 0. Thus the origin O has coordinates $(0, 0)$. This method of associating pairs of real numbers with points has the advantage of associating exactly one pair with each point, and exactly one point of the plane with each ordered pair of real numbers.

Rectangular coordinate systems in space follow the same general pattern as do such systems in the plane. Three mutually perpendicular (intersecting) lines are selected as axes: the x-axis, the y-axis, and the z-axis, with the point of intersection of the three axes being called the origin. Again, a positive direction is chosen arbitrarily on each axis, and the usual correspondence is made between the points of each axis and the real numbers. The zero point on each axis is taken at the origin, and the positive real numbers are on that side of the origin which has been designated as the positive side of the axis.

Following the same pattern of development as in the plane, we consider any point P in space. From P we drop perpendiculars to the axes, and we call P_x, P_y and P_z the feet of these perpendiculars on the x-, y-, and z-axes, respectively (see Figure 26a). The real number associated with P_x on the x-axis is called the x-coordinate of P; the real number associated with P_y on the y-axis becomes the y-coordinate of P; and the real number associated with P_z on the z-axis becomes the z-coordinate of P. If P is on any of the axes, not all the perpendiculars may be drawn. Thus we state further that if P is on the x-axis, its y-coordinate and its x-coordinate are both zero. Similarly, if P is on the y-axis, its x- and z-coordinates are both zero. Finally, the coordinates of the origin are all zero.

It is quite convenient to visualize P (when P is not on an axis) at the corner of a rectangular solid, with the origin O at the opposite corner, as shown in Figure 26b. This may suggest to the reader other approaches he might prefer in finding the coordinates of P, or in locating P if its coordinates are given. For example, suppose we know the coordinates of P. We can then locate P by finding the point on the x-axis that corresponds to its x-coordinate, then moving parallel to the y-axis a distance that corresponds to the y-coordinate of P, and then parallel to the z-axis a distance that corresponds to the z-coordinate of P.

When we designate a point by its coordinates in space, the order of the triple of numbers follows the alphabetic order, that is: (x, y, z). We stated that, in dealing with plane coordinates, it is customary to take the x-axis as

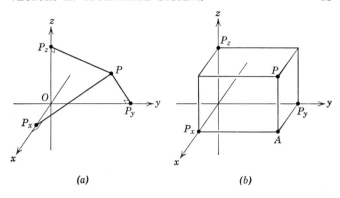

(a)   *(b)*

FIGURE 26

horizontal, etc.   In space, the convention is to have the
positive z-axis pointing upward and the xy-plane horizontal.   It is also customary to have one positive axis
pointing toward us and the other pointing to our right.
However, which axis points toward us and which to our
right   seriously   influences   our   vector   development.
Consequently, before we finally decide on the *orientation*
of the axes, it would be well to explain the notions of
right-handed and *left-handed* triples of vectors.

Let $\{A, B, C\}$ be an *ordered* set of three linearly independent vectors (which can always be considered as
emanating from the same point O).   Since the vectors
are linearly independent, they do not all lie in one plane.
Moreover, no two are on the same or parallel lines.   Thus
the *first* and *second* vectors, A and B, form an angle
θ $(0 < \theta < \pi)$.[1]   Remember!   It's the order of first,

[1] Here, and throughout the entire book, angle measurement is in
terms of radians.   The use of degrees is due to an unfortunate
historical accident and serves to confuse students, especially when
they reach the study of trigonometric functions in calculus.
Because radian measure serves the mathematician in good stead
throughout the whole field of mathematics, we prefer to propa-
gandize by making exclusive use of it.

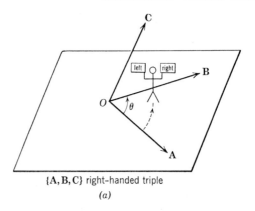

{A, B, C} right-handed triple

(a)

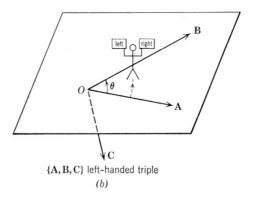

{A, B, C} left-handed triple

(b)

FIGURE 27

second, third in the triple that counts. Now, consider
an observer stationed on the side of the plane of **A** and **B**
that allows him to walk from a point on **A** through the
angle θ to a point on **B**, with his outstretched *right* arm
always pointing away from O (see Figure 27). That is,
he walks about, keeping point O always on his left. If
the observer's head is on the same side of the plane of

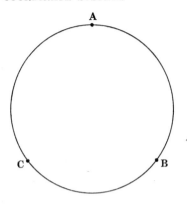

FIGURE 28

A and **B** as the vector **C**, we say {**A**, **B**, **C**} is a *right-handed* or *positive* triple. It should be clear, then, that {**B**, **C**, **A**} and {**C**, **A**, **B**} are also right-handed triples, whereas {**B**, **A**, **C**}, {**A**, **C**, **B**} and {**C**, **B**, **A**} are *left-handed* or *negative* triples. If you think of the vectors as seats at a circular table, all clockwise readings (starting

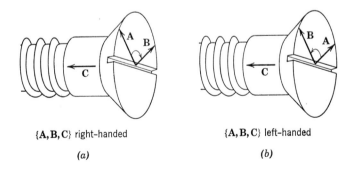

{**A**,**B**,**C**} right-handed   {**A**,**B**,**C**} left-handed

(a)   (b)

FIGURE 29

(a) Ordinary screw goes in. (b) Ordinary screw comes out.

at any letter) yield triples of the same orientation and all counterclockwise readings yield triples of the opposite orientations. This situation is described succinctly by stating that a cyclic permutation of the vectors of a triple does not change its orientation as a left-handed or right-handed triple, as the case may be.

A useful mnemonic is found by studying a screw. Think of the first two vectors of the triple as being on the head of an ordinary (*right-handed*) screw. Turn the first vector into the second through the angle less than π. If this has the effect of driving the screw in the general direction of the third vector, we say the triple is right-handed.

8. BASIS VECTORS AND APPLICATIONS

Let $\mathbf{i}$, $\mathbf{j}$, and $\mathbf{k}$ be three unit vectors in the respective positive x-, y-, and z-directions. We take $\{\mathbf{i}, \mathbf{j}, \mathbf{k}\}$ to be a positive triple, and this establishes the right-handedness of the (x, y, z)-coordinate system. That is, if three vectors in the positive x-, y-, and z-directions form a right-handed triple, we call the (x, y, z)-coordinate system right-handed; otherwise we say it is left-handed (see Figure 30.).

Since $\mathbf{i}$, $\mathbf{j}$, and $\mathbf{k}$ are linearly independent, we know (by Exercise 8, p. 34) that any vector in space can be expressed as a linear combination of them. In particular, let $\mathbf{P} = \overrightarrow{OP}$ where $O = (0, 0, 0)$ and $P = (x, y, z)$; then $\mathbf{P} = x\mathbf{i} + y\mathbf{j} + z\mathbf{k}$. $\mathbf{P}$ is referred to as the *position vector* of point P (see Figure 30c).

We wish to extend our algebra of vectors so that we may work with the *vectors* $\mathbf{i}$, $\mathbf{j}$, and $\mathbf{k}$. To explore addition, subtraction, and multiplication by scalars in this form, let

$$\mathbf{A} = a_1\mathbf{i} + a_2\mathbf{j} + a_3\mathbf{k}$$

and

$$\mathbf{B} = b_1\mathbf{i} + b_2\mathbf{j} + b_3\mathbf{k}.$$

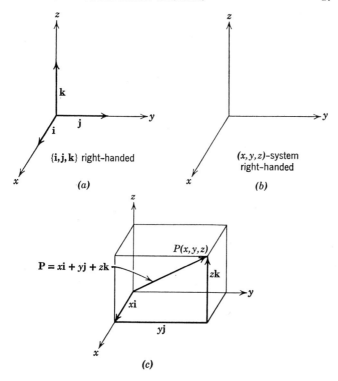

FIGURE 30

Then by Theorem 1,

$$\mathbf{A} + \mathbf{B} = (a_1 + b_1)\mathbf{i} + (a_2 + b_2)\mathbf{j} + (a_3 + b_3)\mathbf{k},$$

and by Theorem 2 (iii)

$$m\mathbf{A} = ma_1\mathbf{i} + ma_2\mathbf{j} + ma_3\mathbf{k},$$

and

$$m\mathbf{A} + n\mathbf{B} = (ma_1 + nb_1)\mathbf{i} + (ma_2 + nb_2)\mathbf{j} \\ + (ma_3 + nb_3)\mathbf{k}.$$

We see, therefore, that sums, scalar multiples, and, in general, linear combinations of vectors expressed in terms of $\mathbf{i}$, $\mathbf{j}$, and $\mathbf{k}$ can also be expressed as linear combinations of vectors $\mathbf{i}$, $\mathbf{j}$, and $\mathbf{k}$. That is, every vector in space can be expressed as a linear combination of these three unit vectors. Mathematicians describe this situation by saying the vectors $\mathbf{i}$, $\mathbf{j}$, and $\mathbf{k}$ *span* or *generate* the space under consideration. Furthermore, the set of vectors $\{\mathbf{i}, \mathbf{j}, \mathbf{k}\}$ is said to serve as a *basis* for the space. *A basis is a linearly independent set that generates the space.* The need for a basis to generate the space is quite clear, but what is the purpose of the stipulation of linear independence? The answer lies in the desire to have a vector expressed in a unique manner relative to a given basis, that is (in our present discussion), if

$$\mathbf{A} = a_1\mathbf{i} + a_2\mathbf{j} + a_3\mathbf{k} = c_1\mathbf{i} + c_2\mathbf{j} + c_3\mathbf{k},$$

we may conclude, as we did earlier, that

$$a_1 = c_1, \quad a_2 = c_2, \quad a_3 = c_3.$$

Suppose, on the other hand, that we used a linearly dependent set $\{\mathbf{i}, \mathbf{j}, \mathbf{k}, \mathbf{h}\}$ to generate the space. Then any vector $\mathbf{V}$ could be written in the form

$$\mathbf{V} = v_1\mathbf{i} + v_2\mathbf{j} + v_3\mathbf{k} + v_4\mathbf{h}. \tag{19}$$

The linear dependence of the set $\{\mathbf{i}, \mathbf{j}, \mathbf{k}, \mathbf{h}\}$ implies the existence of scalars c_1, c_2, c_3, and c_4 (not all zero) such that

$$c_1\mathbf{i} + c_2\mathbf{j} + c_3\mathbf{k} + c_4\mathbf{h} = \mathbf{O}. \tag{20}$$

Adding (19) and (20) yields

$$\mathbf{V} = (v_1 + c_1)\mathbf{i} + (v_2 + c_2)\mathbf{j} + (v_3 + c_3)\mathbf{k} + (v_4 + c_4)\mathbf{h}.$$

Thus, if $\mathbf{h} \neq \mathbf{O}$, we have demonstrated the existence of distinct representations for $\mathbf{V}$ as a linear combination of $\mathbf{i}$, $\mathbf{j}$, $\mathbf{k}$, and $\mathbf{h}$. Actually there are an infinite number of such representations, which can be demonstrated by multiplying (20) by an arbitrary scalar before adding it to (19).

Remark. The reader has no doubt observed that we have avoided any reference to the plane as being two dimensional and space being three dimensional. Our reasoning is in accordance with the thinking of mathematicians who deal with so-called "vector spaces." They do not choose to *assume* any knowledge of the concept of dimension. They see it as naturally related to other concepts involving vectors. In fact, they *define* the dimension of a space—and do so in one of two completely equivalent ways:

(1) The dimension of a space is taken as the number of vectors in a basis for the space. (Of course, this number is shown to be independent of the choice of the basis.)

(2) The dimension of a space is the maximum number of linearly independent vectors in the space.

Consequently, we see that the line would be one dimensional. Theorem 3 and its corollary imply that the plane is two dimensional. Finally, Exercise 8 on p. 34 establishes the three-dimensional character of what we have called "space." The foregoing discussion, which notes that $\mathbf{i}$, $\mathbf{j}$, and $\mathbf{k}$ are linearly independent, and that adding any other vector to this set of three would result in a linearly dependent set, further establishes that "space" is three dimensional.

EXAMPLE 10. Let points be given as follows: $O = (0, 0, 0)$, $A = (1, 3, 4)$, $B = (1, 5, 2)$, $C = (-2, 1, 6)$, $D = (-2, 5, -2)$, and $E = (0, 2, -2)$.

(1) The position vector of point A is given by $\mathbf{A} = \mathbf{i} + 3\mathbf{j} + 4\mathbf{k}$ and the position vector of point E is $\mathbf{E} = 2\mathbf{j} - 2\mathbf{k}$.

(2) How should we write the vector $\overrightarrow{AB}$? Noting Figure 31, we see that $\overrightarrow{AB} = \mathbf{B} - \mathbf{A}$. Hence we write

$$\vec{AB} = (\mathbf{i} + 5\mathbf{j} + 2\mathbf{k}) - (\mathbf{i} + 3\mathbf{j} + 4\mathbf{k})$$
$$= (1 - 1)\mathbf{i} + (5 - 3)\mathbf{j} + (2 - 4)\mathbf{k}$$
$$= 2\mathbf{j} - 2\mathbf{k} = \mathbf{E}.$$

(3) How do we write a vector emanating from O, pointing toward C but half the length of $\mathbf{C}$? We seek $\frac{1}{2}\,\vec{OC}$. This is merely

$$\tfrac{1}{2}\mathbf{C} = \tfrac{1}{2}(-2\mathbf{i} + \mathbf{j} + 6\mathbf{k})$$
$$\tfrac{1}{2}\mathbf{C} = -\mathbf{i} + \tfrac{1}{2}\mathbf{j} + 3\mathbf{k}.$$

(4) How do we write a vector from O to the midpoint of segment BC? Calling M the midpoint of segment BC, we employ Theorem 4 to write

$$\vec{OM} = \mathbf{M} = \tfrac{1}{2}\vec{OB} + \tfrac{1}{2}\vec{OC} \tag{21}$$
$$= \tfrac{1}{2}(\mathbf{i} + 5\mathbf{j} + 2\mathbf{k}) + \tfrac{1}{2}(-2\mathbf{i} + \mathbf{j} + 6\mathbf{k})$$
$$= -\tfrac{1}{2}\mathbf{i} + 3\mathbf{j} + 4\mathbf{k}.$$

Observing that $\mathbf{M}$ is the position vector of M, we can state the coordinates of the midpoint of BC: $M = (-\tfrac{1}{2}, 3, 4)$. This

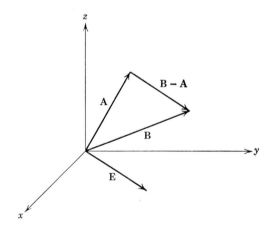

FIGURE 31

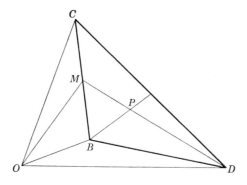

FIGURE 32

procedure can be generalized to find the midpoint of any segment. Call

$$P_1 = (x_1, y_1, z_1) \qquad \text{and} \qquad P_2 = (x_2, y_2, z_2).$$

Then, if M is the midpoint of P_1P_2, we can write

$$\overrightarrow{OM} = \tfrac{1}{2}\overrightarrow{OP}_1 + \tfrac{1}{2}\overrightarrow{OP}_2 = \tfrac{1}{2}(\overrightarrow{OP}_1 + \overrightarrow{OP}_2)$$

$$= \tfrac{1}{2}[(x_1\mathbf{i} + y_1\mathbf{j} + z_1\mathbf{k}) + (x_2\mathbf{i} + y_2\mathbf{j} + z_2\mathbf{k})]$$

$$= \tfrac{1}{2}(x_1 + x_2)\mathbf{i} + \tfrac{1}{2}(y_1 + y_2)\mathbf{j} + \tfrac{1}{2}(z_1 + z_2)\mathbf{k}.$$

Thus the midpoint is

$$M = \left(\frac{x_1 + x_2}{2}, \frac{y_1 + y_2}{2}, \frac{z_1 + z_2}{2} \right).$$

(5) What are the coordinates of the point of intersection of the medians of triangle BCD? Referring to Figure 32, we seek the coordinates of P. Recalling that P divides DM in the ratio 2:1, and using Theorem 4 once again, we write $\overrightarrow{OP} = \tfrac{2}{3}\overrightarrow{OM} + \tfrac{1}{3}\overrightarrow{OD}$. Employing equation 21, we have $\overrightarrow{OP} = \tfrac{2}{3}(\tfrac{1}{2}\overrightarrow{OB} + \tfrac{1}{2}\overrightarrow{OC}) + \tfrac{1}{3}\overrightarrow{OD}$,

or

$$\overrightarrow{OP} = (\tfrac{1}{3})\overrightarrow{OB} + (\tfrac{1}{3})\overrightarrow{OC} + (\tfrac{1}{3})\overrightarrow{OD}. \qquad (22)$$

Consequently,

$$\overrightarrow{OP} = (\tfrac{1}{3})(\mathbf{i} + 5\mathbf{j} + 2\mathbf{k}) + (\tfrac{1}{3})(-2\mathbf{i} + \mathbf{j} + 6\mathbf{k}) \\ + (\tfrac{1}{3})(-2\mathbf{i} + 5\mathbf{j} - 2\mathbf{k}).$$

Then $P = (-1, 11/3, 2)$. It is hardly necessary to state that these methods are valid no matter what the relative positions of the points are. That is, even if O, B, C, and D are in one plane, the formula (22) still holds true.

EXAMPLE 11. Prove that the (radial) vectors drawn from the center of a regular polygon to its vertices sum to the zero vector.

The reader should—before reading the next paragraph—attempt a solution to this problem when the polygon is a triangle, square, and pentagon. He may choose to set the polygon within a coordinate system and perhaps, if necessary, resort to some help from trigonometry or elementary geometry. Before proceeding, the reader should give some thought to the original problem, which does not specify any particular regular polygon but concerns the general case.

Consider the origin of a two-dimensional coordinate system to be at the center of the regular polygon of n sides (see Figure 33). Let $\mathbf{S}$ be the sum of the radial vectors. If $\mathbf{S}$ is not the zero vector, it has a unique inclination of α radius with respect to the x-axis. Rotate the polygon $2\pi/n$ radians about the origin. The sum vector $\mathbf{S}$ is now inclined $\alpha + 2\pi/n$ radians to the x-axis. Since the rotated figure has precisely the same

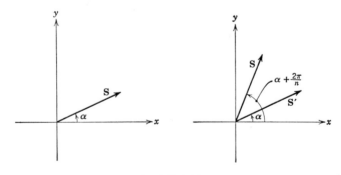

FIGURE 33

appearance on the coordinate system as the unrotated one, the new sum $\mathbf{S}'$ of the radial vectors must again be inclined α radians to the x-axis. Thus we have two vectors $\mathbf{S}$ and $\mathbf{S}'$ inclined differently while both represent the single sum in question. Since we know that the sum vector in unique, i.e., $\mathbf{S} = \mathbf{S}'$, the only compatible solution is the vector $\mathbf{S} = \mathbf{S}' = \mathbf{O}$.

It should be emphasized that it was the *symmetry* of the regular polygon that enabled us to construct this proof. The student of natural science should always be on the lookout for such intrinsic properties that may help to simplify the physical as well as the geometric considerations of his problems. Scientists encounter—and make use of—symmetry in such diverse fields as geometry, algebra, botany, zoology, electrical circuit theory, mechanics, and optics. The reader who wishes to know more about the prominent role played by symmetry in art and science is referred to the fascinating lectures of Hermann Weyl, which are contained in his book, *Symmetry*, Princeton University Press. A portion of Weyl's book is reproduced in *The World of Mathematics* by James R. Newman.

EXERCISES

1. (*a*) Locate on a sheet of graph paper the points $A = (6, 4, 10)$, $B = (-6, 4, -10)$, $C = (4, -6, -10)$, and $D = (0, 10, 4)$.

(*b*) Write the position vectors $\mathbf{A}$, $\mathbf{B}$, $\mathbf{C}$, and $\mathbf{D}$ in terms of the $\{\mathbf{i}, \mathbf{j}, \mathbf{k}\}$-basis.

(*c*) Find the sum $\mathbf{A} + \mathbf{B} + \mathbf{C} + \mathbf{D}$ graphically, and check this against the computation in the $\{\mathbf{i}, \mathbf{j}, \mathbf{k}\}$-system.

(*d*) Compute $\mathbf{A} - \mathbf{B}$, $\mathbf{D} - \mathbf{C}$, $\overrightarrow{BD}$, and $\overrightarrow{AC}$.

(*e*) Find the midpoint of segment AB.

(*f*) Find the coordinates of the point X that divides segment AB in the ratio $2: -1$.

(*g*) Find the coordinates of the point Y so that B is the midpoint of segment AY.

(*h*) Find the median point of the triangle ABD.

2. Let $\mathbf{A} = 2\mathbf{i} - 4\mathbf{j}$, $\mathbf{B} = -\mathbf{i} - 2\mathbf{j}$, $\mathbf{C} = \mathbf{i} + \mathbf{j} + 3\mathbf{k}$, and $\mathbf{D} = 2\mathbf{i} - 3\mathbf{j} + \mathbf{k}$.

    (*a*) Determine $2\mathbf{A}$ as a linear combination of $\mathbf{i}$, $\mathbf{j}$, and $\mathbf{k}$.

    (*b*) Determine $-3\mathbf{B}$ as a linear combination of $\mathbf{i}$, $\mathbf{j}$, and $\mathbf{k}$.

    (*c*) Determine $3\mathbf{B} - 2\mathbf{A}$ as a linear combination of $\mathbf{i}$, $\mathbf{j}$, and $\mathbf{k}$.

    (*d*) Find $\mathbf{A} + \mathbf{B} - \mathbf{C}$ as a linear combination of $\mathbf{i}$, $\mathbf{j}$, and $\mathbf{k}$.

    (*e*) Is $\{\mathbf{A}, \mathbf{B}, \mathbf{C}\}$ a linearly dependent set?

    (*f*) Is $\{\mathbf{A}, \mathbf{B}, \mathbf{C}, \mathbf{D}\}$ a linearly dependent set?

    (*g*) Let $OAXC$ be a parallelogram, with $O = (0, 0, 0)$, $A = (2, -4, 0)$, and $C = (1, 1, 3)$. Find the fourth vertex. (*Hint:* How is the sum of two vectors related to a parallelogram?)

3. Do the position vectors $\mathbf{A}$, $\mathbf{B}$, and $\mathbf{C}$ of Exercise 1 form a linearly dependent set?

4. Let $\mathbf{A} = \mathbf{i} - \mathbf{j}$, $\mathbf{B} = \mathbf{i} + \mathbf{j}$, and $\mathbf{C} = \mathbf{j} - \mathbf{k}$.

    (*a*) Is $\{\mathbf{A}, \mathbf{B}, \mathbf{C}\}$ a linearly dependent set?

    (*b*) Express the vector $\mathbf{V} = 2\mathbf{i} + 4\mathbf{j} - \mathbf{k}$ as a linear combination of $\mathbf{A}$, $\mathbf{B}$, and $\mathbf{C}$.

5. (*a*) Prove that the sum of the eight vectors from the center of a cube to the vertices is the zero vector. Do this by assigning coordinates to the vertices, writing the eight vectors explicitly, and then summing.

    (*b*) Let $\mathfrak{D}$ be a regular dodecahedron (12 faces) and $\mathfrak{S}$ its circumscribed sphere. Prove that the sum of the vectors from the center of $\mathfrak{S}$ to the vertices of $\mathfrak{D}$ is the zero vector. How many such radial vectors are there? (You might look this up in a solid geometry text.)

9. THE COMPLEX PLANE

A two-dimensional space that naturally admits to analysis in terms of vectors is the complex plane, which may be familiar to the reader from his studies in algebra and trigonometry. In order to see the complex plane from the vector point of view, consider a rectangular coordinate system with a basis consisting of two unit vectors: $\mathbf{1}$ and $\mathbf{i}$. $\mathbf{1}$ is taken in the positive x-direction and $\mathbf{i}$ in the positive y-direction (see Figure 34). The unit vector $\mathbf{i}$ is actually the imaginary unit $i = \sqrt{-1}$.

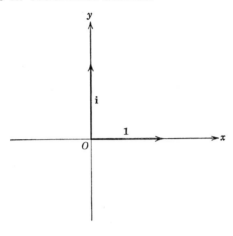

FIGURE 34

That is, the role of basis vector **i** (of Section 8) is now played by **1**, and the role of **j** is now played by **i**.

$$
\begin{array}{cc}
\text{Old} & \text{New} \\
\mathbf{i} & = & 1 \\
\mathbf{j} & = & \mathbf{i}
\end{array}
$$

If $P = (x, y)$, the vector $\overrightarrow{OP} = x\mathbf{1} + y\mathbf{i}$, or, more simply, the vector $\overrightarrow{OP}$ may be thought of as the complex number $x + iy$. Thus every complex number is actually a vector in the plane. If scalars are taken to be real numbers, the multiplication of vectors by scalars corresponds precisely to multiplication of complex numbers by real numbers (see Exercise 2, page 57). Is it also true that vector addition corresponds to addition of complex numbers? To answer this question we consider two complex numbers: $c_1 = x_1 + iy_1$ and $c_2 = x_2 + iy_2$, their related vectors being $\mathbf{c_1} = x_1\mathbf{1} + y_1\mathbf{i}$ and $\mathbf{c_2} =$

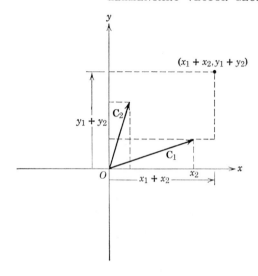

FIGURE 35

$x_2\mathbf{1} + y_2\mathbf{i}$. Addition of complex numbers allows us to say

$$c_1 + c_2 = (x_1 + x_2) + i(y_1 + y_2);$$

and addition of vectors permits us to write

$$\mathbf{c}_1 + \mathbf{c}_2 = (x_1 + x_2)\mathbf{1} + (y_1 + y_2)\mathbf{i}.$$

Thus we see that $c_1 + c_2$ corresponds to the vector $\mathbf{c}_1 + \mathbf{c}_2$.

EXAMPLE 12. Considering Example 11 in the light of this vector approach to the complex plane, we can reach an extremely simple and elegant solution.

Let the regular polygon be centered at the origin, with one of its radial vectors lying on the x-axis. Figure 36 illustrates the approach for the pentagon. If the radial vectors are chosen of unit length, we know from algebra that the n vectors, as complex numbers, are simply the solutions of the equation

$x^n = 1$. But the sum of the roots of this equation is zero, for the coefficient of the x^{n-1} term is zero. This completes the proof.

EXERCISES

1. Sketch the vectors representing the complex numbers $2 - i$ and $3 + 2i$. Give a construction for their addition and subtraction, and compare this geometric view of the operations with the algebraic.

2. Exhibit the following scalar multiples of $2 - i$:

$$2(2 - i), \quad \tfrac{3}{2}(2 - i), \quad \tfrac{1}{2}(2 - i), \quad -(2 - i), \quad -2(2 - i).$$

What geometric fact can one deduce about the set of (real) scalar multiples of a complex number?

Remark on Length and Absolute Value. From our brief discussion of complex numbers as vectors we can gain some insight regarding the symbolism $|\ \ |$, which is used to denote the absolute value of a real or complex

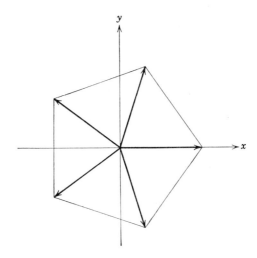

FIGURE 36

number as well as the length of a vector. The two notions, absolute value and length, are actually interrelated, or, more accurately stated, *the notion of absolute value is a special case of the length of a vector.* This is the basis for the same choice of symbolism.

The *absolute value* or *modulus* of a complex number $a + bi$, written $|a + bi|$, is defined as $\sqrt{a^2 + b^2}$. But if we view the complex number as a vector in the complex plane (see Figure 37), then the length of $\mathbf{V} = a\mathbf{1} + b\mathbf{i}$ can be determined by the Pythagorean theorem

$$|a\mathbf{1} + b\mathbf{i}| = \sqrt{a^2 + b^2} = |a + bi|.$$

In the event that we are dealing with real numbers, we may treat them as a subset $R^{\#}$ of the complex numbers. That is,

$$R^{\#} = \{a + bi | b = 0\}.$$

Thus the length of $\mathbf{r} = a\mathbf{1} + 0\mathbf{i}$ is $|\mathbf{r}| = \sqrt{a^2} = |a|$. In both cases we see that the absolute value of a number

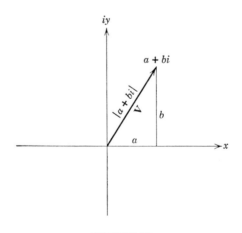

FIGURE 37

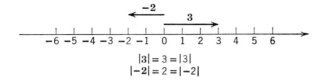

$$|3| = 3 = |3|$$
$$|-2| = 2 = |-2|$$

FIGURE 38

is merely the length of the vector associated with that number. One may also consider the real numbers as constituting a one-dimensional space, i.e., as a line (see Figure 38), with the same result: absolute value of the real number equals length of the vector.

From this geometric view of absolute value one can see the plausibility of the following properties of absolute value:

(i) $|a| = |-a| \geq 0$

(ii) $|a + b| \leq |a| + |b|$

(iii) $|a| - |b| \leq |a + b|$

(iv) $||a| - |b|| \leq |a - b|.$

EXERCISE

1. Considering a and b to be complex numbers, give geometric interpretations of the algebraic properties (i) through (iv) above.

3

inner
products

10. DEFINITION

In this chapter we begin to introduce quantitative aspects into our vector algebra. Of particular interest are the notions of distance and angle. In order to see how best to introduce such concepts, it might be advisable to have a look at them in the framework of coordinate geometry.

Since the plane is more easily dealt with than three dimensions, we let $A = (a_1, a_2)$ and $B = (b_1, b_2)$ be points in the (x, y)-plane (Figure 39). The distance d, between A and B, which we denote $|AB|$, can be found (by the Pythagorean theorem) from the formula

$$d^2 = (a_1 - b_1)^2 + (a_2 - b_2)^2, \tag{23}$$

or $$d = \sqrt{(a_1 - b_1)^2 + (a_2 - b_2)^2}. \tag{23a}$$

Note that it makes no difference whether A or B is considered first, for d is also equal to

$$\sqrt{(b_1 - a_1)^2 + (b_2 - a_2)^2}.$$

Expanding (23) results in

$$d^2 = a_1{}^2 + a_2{}^2 + b_1{}^2 + b_2{}^2 - 2(a_1b_1 + a_2b_2). \quad (24)$$

If we introduce—for convenience in the present discussion—the notation $A*B = a_1b_1 + a_2b_2$, we can rewrite (24) as

$$|AB|^2 = A*A + B*B - 2A*B. \quad (25)$$

Hence we have distance between two points described completely in terms of the symbol * (and, of course, + and −).

Turning to angle measurement, we examine Figure 39a, seeking an expression for the angle θ. By the law of cosines we write

$$|AB|^2 = |OA|^2 + |OB|^2 - 2|OA|\,|OB|\cos\theta;$$

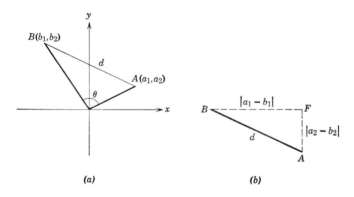

(a) (b)

FIGURE 39

Note. In (b) above, it is possible that $a - b$ is positive, negative, or zero. We therefore designate the distance (non-negative) between A and F (also B and F) by absolute value in order to assure the non-negative character of distance. Consequently (23a) can be written $d = \sqrt{|a_1 - b_1|^2 + |a_2 - b_2|^2}$.

or, using our * notation,

$$|AB|^2 = A*A + B*B - 2\sqrt{A*A}\,\sqrt{B*B}\cos\theta. \quad (26)$$

Upon subtracting (26) from (25) and simplifying, we find

$$\cos\theta = \frac{A*B}{\sqrt{A*A}\,\sqrt{B*B}}, \quad (27)$$

so we see that angles can also be expressed in terms of the * notation.

Drawing motivation from this discussion—primarily from (27)—we start afresh with vectors (not restricted to two dimensions) and define the *inner product* of **A** and **B** as

$$\mathbf{A} \cdot \mathbf{B} = |\mathbf{A}|\,|\mathbf{B}|\cos\theta, \quad (28)$$

where θ is the angle between the two vectors when they are arranged to emanate from the same point. Accordingly, the notions of distance (length) and angle are both incorporated in our definition of inner product. Note that it is immaterial whether θ, $-\theta$, or $2\pi - \theta$ is chosen, for $\cos\theta = \cos(-\theta) = \cos(2\pi - \theta)$. (See Figure 40.)

Because of the notation employed, the inner product is also called the *dot product*. Still another name is the

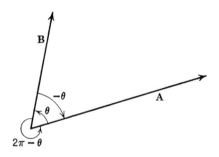

FIGURE 40

scalar product, for this method of "multiplying" two vectors yields a scalar (examine equations 28). All these terminologies enjoy popularity in mathematics and physics textbooks, so we shall employ them all in order that the reader may feel at home with any one.

Two immediate corollaries to the definition are

$$\mathbf{A} \cdot \mathbf{B} = \mathbf{B} \cdot \mathbf{A} \qquad \text{(commutativity of dot product)}$$

and $\qquad \mathbf{A} \cdot \mathbf{A} = |\mathbf{A}|^2 \qquad$ (since $\cos 0 = 1$).

If **A** is perpendicular to **B**, $\mathbf{A} \cdot \mathbf{B} = 0$. (Why?) However, if $\mathbf{A} \cdot \mathbf{B} = 0$, there are three possibilities:

> (1) $\mathbf{A} = \mathbf{O}$,
>
> (2) $\mathbf{B} = \mathbf{O}$,
>
> (3) **A** is perpendicular to **B**.

If we agree that the zero vector is perpendicular to every vector (see page 22 for justification of this convention), we can combine these conclusions in a single statement:
Theorem 5. *If* **A** *is perpendicular to* **B,** *then* $\mathbf{A} \cdot \mathbf{B} = 0$; *and conversely, if* $\mathbf{A} \cdot \mathbf{B} = 0$, *then* **A** *is perpendicular to* **B**.

Word of Caution. Many beginning students have difficulty in believing that vectors in space are perpendicular if they do not intersect. It must therefore be emphasized once again that the definition of equality of vectors permits us to move a free vector as long as it is kept parallel to its original position; this enables us to think of any two vectors as intersecting. It is the sincere hope of the author that the reader has long since understood this point and hence is thoroughly bored with the word of caution.

11. PROPERTIES OF INNER PRODUCT

An examination of Figure 41 leads to an interesting geometric interpretation of the inner product. From

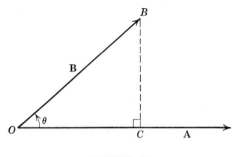

FIGURE 41

triangle OCB we see that $\cos \theta = \dfrac{\left|\overrightarrow{OC}\right|}{\left|\overrightarrow{OB}\right|}$ or

$$\left|\overrightarrow{OC}\right| = \left|\overrightarrow{OB}\right| \cos \theta.$$

Since $\overrightarrow{OB} = \mathbf{B}$ and $\overrightarrow{OC}$ is the "vector projection" of $\mathbf{B}$ on $\mathbf{A}$, we write

$$\text{projection of } \mathbf{B} \text{ on } \mathbf{A} = \left|\mathbf{B}\right| \cos \theta,^{[1]} \qquad (29)$$

which smacks of the inner product $\mathbf{A} \cdot \mathbf{B}$. In fact, multiplying by $\left|\mathbf{A}\right|$ results in the right member of (29) becoming $\mathbf{A} \cdot \mathbf{B}$. That is,

$$\left|\mathbf{A}\right| \,(\text{projection of } \mathbf{B} \text{ on } \mathbf{A}) = \left|\mathbf{A}\right| \left|\mathbf{B}\right| \cos \theta = \mathbf{A} \cdot \mathbf{B}, \qquad (30)$$

which gives us a geometric association with the inner product concept.

Before proceeding, we must clarify the ideas contained in (30). The reader may feel—and rightly so—that perhaps too much has been inferred from a rather special picture. We therefore provide the following definition.

---

[1] Note that (29) gives the projection of one vector upon another as a scalar, which may be positive, negative, or zero.

Definition. *By the projection of* **B** *on* **A**, *written* $pr_A\mathbf{B}$, *we mean the orthogonal projection of* **B** *on the line of action of* **A**. *The* $pr_A\mathbf{B}$ *is obtained by dropping perpendiculars from the origin and endpoint of* **B** *to the line of action of* **A** (*see Figure 42*). *The distance between the feet of these perpendiculars is the magnitude of the* $pr_A\mathbf{B}$. *If the angle* θ *between* **A** *and* **B** (*when* **A** *and* **B** *are arranged to emanate from the same point*) *is acute, then* $pr_A\mathbf{B}$ *is positive; if* θ *is obtuse then* $pr_A\mathbf{B}$ *is negative.*

Now that the notion of projecting one vector upon another has been made precise, we restate (30) as

Theorem 6. $\mathbf{A} \cdot \mathbf{B} = (pr_B\mathbf{A})|\mathbf{B}| = (pr_A\mathbf{B})|\mathbf{A}|.$

The completion of the proof is left as an exercise for the reader.

From this result we prove that *the inner product is distributive with respect to addition,* which we state as

Theorem 7. $\mathbf{A} \cdot (\mathbf{B} + \mathbf{C}) = \mathbf{A} \cdot \mathbf{B} + \mathbf{A} \cdot \mathbf{C}.$

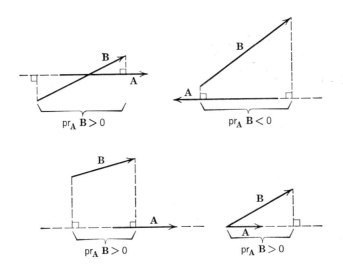

FIGURE 42

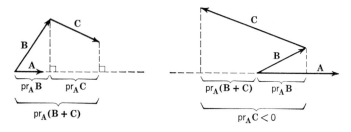

FIGURE 43

Proof. (See Figure 43.)

$\mathbf{A} \cdot (\mathbf{B} + \mathbf{C})$
$= \text{pr}_{\mathbf{A}}(\mathbf{B} + \mathbf{C})|\mathbf{A}|$ (by Theorem 6)
$= (\text{pr}_{\mathbf{A}}\mathbf{B} + \text{pr}_{\mathbf{A}}\mathbf{C})|\mathbf{A}|$ (justify!)
$= (\text{pr}_{\mathbf{A}}\mathbf{B})|\mathbf{A}| + (\text{pr}_{\mathbf{A}}\mathbf{C})|\mathbf{A}|$
$= \mathbf{A} \cdot \mathbf{B} + \mathbf{A} \cdot \mathbf{C}$ (by using Theorem 6 once again).

Corollary.

$$(\mathbf{A} + \mathbf{B}) \cdot (\mathbf{C} + \mathbf{D}) = \mathbf{A} \cdot \mathbf{C} + \mathbf{A} \cdot \mathbf{D} + \mathbf{B} \cdot \mathbf{C} + \mathbf{B} \cdot \mathbf{D}.$$

Proof. By Theorem 7 we write

$$(\mathbf{A} + \mathbf{B}) \cdot (\mathbf{C} + \mathbf{D}) = (\mathbf{A} + \mathbf{B}) \cdot \mathbf{C} + (\mathbf{A} + \mathbf{B}) \cdot \mathbf{D},$$

and leave the remainder of the proof for the reader.

EXAMPLE 13. We prove by vector methods that the perpendicular bisectors of a triangle meet in a point.

Because vectors may be "moved," we adopt what may seem to be a strange approach. The reader should become familiar with it, for such an approach is extremely useful when several lines meeting in a point must be shown.

Let the triangle be ABC, with the perpendicular bisectors of AB and BC meeting in point O (see Figure 44). Let M, N, and P be the midpoints of sides AB, BC, and AC, respectively. The approach we adopt is to show that OP is actually perpendicular to AC.

We begin by stating the hypothesis in vector language.

$$\overrightarrow{OM} \cdot \overrightarrow{AB} = 0 \text{ (by Theorem 5, for } \overrightarrow{OM} \perp \overrightarrow{AB}). \quad (31)$$

Rewriting (31), using the fact that M is the midpoint of AB, we get

$$(\tfrac{1}{2}\mathbf{A} + \tfrac{1}{2}\mathbf{B}) \cdot (\mathbf{B} - \mathbf{A}) = 0,$$

which, expanded according to the corollary of Theorem 7, becomes

$$\tfrac{1}{2}\mathbf{B} \cdot \mathbf{B} - \tfrac{1}{2}\mathbf{A} \cdot \mathbf{A} = 0.$$

Hence $\mathbf{A} \cdot \mathbf{A} = \mathbf{B} \cdot \mathbf{B}$, which expresses the fact that the length of $\mathbf{A}$ equals the length of $\mathbf{B}$. We leave it to the reader to show in a similar manner that

$$\mathbf{B} \cdot \mathbf{B} = \mathbf{C} \cdot \mathbf{C}.$$

Now what must be shown is that $\overrightarrow{OP}$ is perpendicular to $\overrightarrow{AC}$, which expressed vectorially is

$$\mathbf{P} \cdot (\mathbf{C} - \mathbf{A}) = 0.$$

We therefore expand $\mathbf{P} \cdot (\mathbf{C} - \mathbf{A})$, using relations from our hypothesis in the hopes of showing this dot product to be

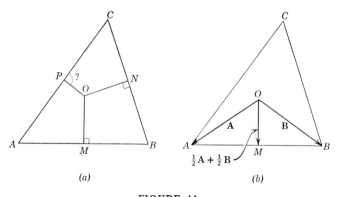

(a)   *(b)*

FIGURE 44

zero. Thus

$$\mathbf{P} \cdot (\mathbf{C} - \mathbf{A}) = (\tfrac{1}{2}\mathbf{A} + \tfrac{1}{2}\mathbf{C}) \cdot (\mathbf{C} - \mathbf{A})$$
$$= \tfrac{1}{2}\mathbf{C} \cdot \mathbf{C} - \tfrac{1}{2}\mathbf{A} \cdot \mathbf{A}.$$

Thus $\qquad \mathbf{P} \cdot (\mathbf{C} - \mathbf{A}) = 0$ (for $\mathbf{A} \cdot \mathbf{A} = \mathbf{C} \cdot \mathbf{C}$),

from which we conclude the desired result.

This example illustrates once again the fact that a judicious selection of the point from which the several vectors are considered to emanate often leads to a simple solution to an otherwise difficult problem.

12. COMPONENTS

In the study of mechanics it is frequently useful—and often necessary—to consider a single vector as the sum or resultant of two other vectors. For example, in pushing a lawn mower (see Figure 45a), the force $\mathbf{F}$ is exerted along the bar of the mower, but the questions asked in physics are: What is the force $\mathbf{F}_h$ that contributes

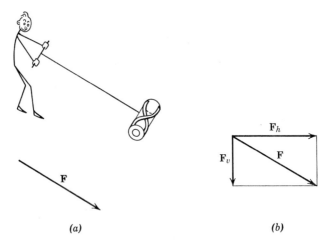

(a)   (b)

FIGURE 45

to the horizontal motion of the mower? And, what force $\mathbf{F}_v$ is "wasted" by being applied vertically downward? These questions are answered by considering $\mathbf{F}$ as the sum of $\mathbf{F}_h$ and $\mathbf{F}_v$ (Figure 45b). $\mathbf{F}_h$ is called the horizontal *component* of $\mathbf{F}$, and $\mathbf{F}_v$ is called the vertical component of $\mathbf{F}$. The problem of determining the components is a problem in dot products as is easily seen by noting that the magnitude of a component is the magnitude of the projection of $\mathbf{F}$. For example, $|\mathbf{F}_h| = |\mathbf{F}| \, |\cos \theta|$, and this relation can easily be transformed into a dot product by making use of a unit vector $\mathbf{U}$ along the horizontal. Then $|\mathbf{F}_h| = |\mathbf{F} \cdot \mathbf{U}|$, and we may further write

$$\mathbf{F}_h = (\mathbf{F} \cdot \mathbf{U})\mathbf{U} \qquad (32)$$

The unit vector $\mathbf{U}$ serves as a "gimmick" in two capacities. First, to assist us in writing the magnitude of a component in the language of dot product; and second, it enables us to write $\mathbf{F}_h$ explicitly as a vector because $\mathbf{U}$ itself, in (32), imparts a direction to the right member while it does not distort the magnitude.[2]

EXAMPLE 14. In plotting wind forces on plane graph paper (Figure 46) it is found that the wind force, at present, is vector $\mathbf{F} = 3\mathbf{i} + 4\mathbf{j}$ ($\mathbf{i}$ and $\mathbf{j}$ are basis vectors in the xy-plane). We shall express, in terms of scalar products: (1) the magnitude of $\mathbf{F}$; (2) the component of $\mathbf{F}$ in the direction of the x-axis; (3) the component of $\mathbf{F}$ along the y-axis; and (4) the component of $\mathbf{F}$ along vector $\mathbf{A} = -\mathbf{i} + 5\mathbf{j}$.

(1) $|\mathbf{F}| = \sqrt{\mathbf{F} \cdot \mathbf{F}} = \sqrt{(3\mathbf{i} + 4\mathbf{j}) \cdot (3\mathbf{i} + 4\mathbf{j})}$

(2) $\mathbf{F}_x = (\mathbf{F} \cdot \mathbf{i})\mathbf{i} = [(3\mathbf{i} + 4\mathbf{j}) \cdot \mathbf{i}]\mathbf{i}$

---

[2] Some authors prefer to define components as scalars rather than as vectors. This is purely a matter of taste, which is often colored by pragmatic considerations. Readers of mathematical literature would do well to heed the advice given to Alice by Humpty Dumpty: "When I use a word, it means just what I choose it to mean—neither more nor less."

(3) $\mathbf{F}_y = (\mathbf{F} \cdot \mathbf{j})\mathbf{j} = [(3\mathbf{i} + 4\mathbf{j}) \cdot \mathbf{j}]\mathbf{j}$

(4) The unit vector along $\mathbf{A}$ is $\dfrac{\mathbf{A}}{|\mathbf{A}|}$. Thus the component

of $\mathbf{F}$ that we seek is

$$\mathbf{F}_a = \left(\mathbf{F} \cdot \frac{\mathbf{A}}{|\mathbf{A}|}\right)\frac{\mathbf{A}}{|\mathbf{A}|} = (\mathbf{F} \cdot \mathbf{A})\frac{\mathbf{A}}{|\mathbf{A}|^2} = (\mathbf{F} \cdot \mathbf{A})\frac{\mathbf{A}}{\mathbf{A} \cdot \mathbf{A}}$$

$$= ((3\mathbf{i} + 4\mathbf{j}) \cdot (-\mathbf{i} + 5\mathbf{j}))\frac{-\mathbf{i} + 5\mathbf{j}}{(-\mathbf{i} + 5\mathbf{j}) \cdot (-\mathbf{i} + 5\mathbf{j})}.$$

13. INNER PRODUCT FORMULAS

The form of the answers in Example 14 is quite cumbersome and of such a nature that it is difficult for anyone to gain any insight from the answers. We therefore turn

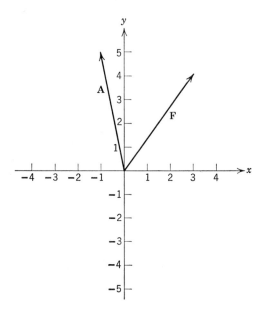

FIGURE 46

attention to simplifying those expressions that involve the inner product of vectors in terms of their rectangular components (in the directions of the rectangular axes). We shall take advantage of the fact that vectors in space are generally no more difficult to handle than vectors in a plane. Thus our computations will deal directly with vectors in three dimensions, admitting the possibility of **i**, **j**, and **k** components.

First, we note the fact that the length of the basis vectors is one implies $\sqrt{\mathbf{i} \cdot \mathbf{i}} = \sqrt{\mathbf{j} \cdot \mathbf{j}} = \sqrt{\mathbf{k} \cdot \mathbf{k}} = 1$. Hence

$$\mathbf{i} \cdot \mathbf{i} = \mathbf{j} \cdot \mathbf{j} = \mathbf{k} \cdot \mathbf{k} = 1. \tag{33}$$

Secondly, we observe that

$$\mathbf{i} \cdot \mathbf{j} = \mathbf{j} \cdot \mathbf{k} = \mathbf{k} \cdot \mathbf{i} = 0, \tag{34}$$

which follows from the mutual perpendicularity of **i**, **j**, and **k**. Now, let

$$\mathbf{A} = a_1\mathbf{i} + a_2\mathbf{j} + a_3\mathbf{k} \qquad \text{and} \qquad \mathbf{B} = b_1\mathbf{i} + b_2\mathbf{j} + b_3\mathbf{k}.$$

Then, making use of Theorem 7 (and its corollary), (33) and (34), we compute as follows:

$$\begin{aligned}
\mathbf{A} \cdot \mathbf{B} &= (a_1\mathbf{i} + a_2\mathbf{j} + a_3\mathbf{k}) \cdot (b_1\mathbf{i} + b_2\mathbf{j} + b_3\mathbf{k}) \\
&= a_1\mathbf{i} \cdot b_1\mathbf{i} + a_1\mathbf{i} \cdot b_2\mathbf{j} + a_1\mathbf{i} \cdot b_3\mathbf{k} \\
&\quad + a_2\mathbf{j} \cdot b_1\mathbf{i} + a_2\mathbf{j} \cdot b_2\mathbf{j} + a_2\mathbf{j} \cdot b_3\mathbf{k} \\
&\quad + a_3\mathbf{k} \cdot b_1\mathbf{i} + a_3\mathbf{k} \cdot b_2\mathbf{j} + a_3\mathbf{k} \cdot b_3\mathbf{k} \\
&= a_1\mathbf{i} \cdot b_1\mathbf{i} + a_2\mathbf{j} \cdot b_2\mathbf{j} + a_3\mathbf{k} \cdot b_3\mathbf{k}.
\end{aligned}$$

Finally, we have a simple formula for the inner product of two vectors:

$$\mathbf{A} \cdot \mathbf{B} = a_1b_1 + a_2b_2 + a_3b_3. \tag{35}$$

The length of **A** can now be found by the formula

$$|\mathbf{A}| = \sqrt{\mathbf{A} \cdot \mathbf{A}} = \sqrt{a_1{}^2 + a_2{}^2 + a_3{}^2}. \tag{36}$$

From the definition of $\mathbf{A} \cdot \mathbf{B}$, (35) and (36), we solve for cosine of the angle between $\mathbf{A}$ and $\mathbf{B}$, getting

$$\cos \theta = \frac{a_1 b_1 + a_2 b_2 + a_3 b_3}{\sqrt{a_1{}^2 + a_2{}^2 + a_3{}^2} \sqrt{b_1{}^2 + b_2{}^2 + b_3{}^2}}. \quad (37)$$

(Note that (35) and (36) are precisely the formulas used in our heuristic reasoning on pages 60-62, where we were informally exploring a method for introducing quantitative aspects into our vector algebra.)

EXAMPLE 15. We return to Example 14 to make explicit computations of the answers given there in unsimplified form.

(1) $|\mathbf{F}| = \sqrt{3 \cdot 3 + 4 \cdot 4} = 5$

(2) $\mathbf{F}_x = [(3 \cdot 1) + (4 \cdot 0)]\mathbf{i} = 3\mathbf{i}.$

(3) $\mathbf{F}_y = [(3 \cdot 0) + (4 \cdot 1)]\mathbf{j} = 4\mathbf{j}.$

(4) $\mathbf{F}_a = (3(-1) + 4 \cdot 5) \dfrac{-\mathbf{i} + 5\mathbf{j}}{(-1)(-1) + 5 \cdot 5}$

$$= \frac{17}{26} (-\mathbf{i} + 5\mathbf{j}).$$

We now ask the question: What is the angle α between $\mathbf{F}$ and $\mathbf{A}$ of Example 14?

Using (37), we write

$$\cos \alpha = \frac{\mathbf{F} \cdot \mathbf{A}}{\sqrt{\mathbf{F} \cdot \mathbf{F}} \sqrt{\mathbf{A} \cdot \mathbf{A}}}$$

$$= \frac{(3\mathbf{i} + 4\mathbf{j}) \cdot (-\mathbf{i} + 5\mathbf{j})}{\sqrt{3 \cdot 3 + 4 \cdot 4} \sqrt{(-1)(-1) + 5 \cdot 5}}$$

$$= \frac{-3 + 20}{5 \sqrt{26}} = \frac{17}{5 \sqrt{26}};$$

or

$$\cos \alpha = \frac{17 \sqrt{26}}{130}.$$

If we were interested in a precise value for α in terms of degrees or radians, it would now be a simple matter to find α by consulting a table for the values of the cosine function.

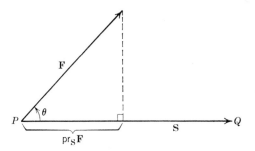

FIGURE 47

14. WORK

The work done in applying a force of magnitude f through a distance s is defined by physicists to be the product fs. Thus work is done if and only if motion occurs. Furthermore, it should be emphasized that *only that force which produces the motion is used to compute the work done.* If we have a force vector **F** applied to an object (see Figure 47) with the effect of moving the object along a straight line from P to Q, the force used to compute the work done is that of the *component of* **F** (along PQ). That is, calling $\mathbf{S} = \overrightarrow{PQ}$,

$$W = (\mathrm{pr_S F})|\mathbf{S}|. \tag{38}$$

(We write (38) in terms of the projection of **F** to allow the possibility of work being negative. Although negative work may sound strange to the uninitiated, the concept is one of great practical value to the physicist and engineer, who need it for an adequate mathematical formulation of the fundamental laws of mechanics and electricity.)

But formula (38) can be rewritten

$$W = |\mathbf{F}|\cos\theta|\mathbf{S}|;$$

or, finally,

$$W = \mathbf{F} \cdot \mathbf{S},$$

which expresses the idea that *dot product can be viewed as work done by one vector in the direction of the other;* or perhaps the reader might prefer to view work as a physical interpretation of the dot product.

EXERCISES

1. Using the approach of Example 13, prove that the medians of a triangle meet in a point. That is, let AM and BN be two medians of triangle ABC, and call P their point of intersection; then show that the extension of CP actually bisects side AB.

2. Let ABC be a right triangle with hypotenuse BC, and D on BC be the foot of the perpendicular from A. Consider one force of magnitude $\dfrac{1}{\left|\overrightarrow{AB}\right|}$ acting in the direction of $\overrightarrow{AB}$, and another of magnitude $\dfrac{1}{\left|\overrightarrow{AC}\right|}$ acting in the direction $\overrightarrow{AC}$. Prove that the resultant is a force of magnitude $\dfrac{1}{\left|\overrightarrow{AD}\right|}$ acting in the direction of $\overrightarrow{AD}$. (*Hint.* Use components.)

3. Find a vector perpendicular to $\mathbf{V} = 2\mathbf{i} - 3\mathbf{j}$ and whose length is four times the length of $\mathbf{V}$.

4. The coordinates of two points are $(3, 1, 2)$ and $(2, -2, 4)$. Find the cosine of the angle between the vectors joining the origin to these points.

5. Prove that the sum of the squares of the diagonals of a parallelogram is equal to the sum of the squares of the sides.

6. Prove that the sum of the squares of the sides of any (not necessarily plane) quadrilateral exceeds the sum of the squares of the diagonals by four times the square of the line segment that joins the midpoints of the diagonals.

7. By means of dot products prove that an angle inscribed in a semicircle is a right angle. (If AB is a diameter, O the center,

and P any point on the circle, then $\overrightarrow{OB} = -\overrightarrow{OA}$. Evaluate the dot product $\overrightarrow{AP} \cdot \overrightarrow{BP}$.)

8. Prove that the altitudes of a triangle meet in a point. (*Hint.* Use the approach of Example 13, and rely heavily on Theorem 5.)

9. Prove that if two circles intersect, the line joining their centers is perpendicular to the line joining their points of intersection.

10. Let
$$\mathbf{A} = 2\mathbf{i} - 3\mathbf{j} + 4\mathbf{k}$$
$$\mathbf{B} = -2\mathbf{i} + \mathbf{j} - \mathbf{k}.$$

   (a) Find $\mathbf{A} \cdot \mathbf{B}$.
   (b) Find $\mathrm{pr_B}\,\mathbf{A}$ and $\mathrm{pr_A}\,\mathbf{B}$.
   (c) Find the component of $\mathbf{A}$ along $\mathbf{B}$.
   (d) Find the work done by force vector $\mathbf{A}$ in moving a particle from the origin to $(2, 0, 0)$ along the x-axis.
   (e) Find the work done by $\mathbf{A}$ in moving a particle from the origin to $(1, 2, -1)$.

11. Let $\mathbf{F}$ be the sum of n forces $\mathbf{F}_1, \mathbf{F}_2, \ldots, \mathbf{F}_n$, all acting at the point O. Then

$$W = \mathbf{F} \cdot \mathbf{S} = \mathbf{F}_1 \cdot \mathbf{S} + \mathbf{F}_2 \cdot \mathbf{S} + \cdots + \mathbf{F}_n \cdot \mathbf{S}. \quad \text{(Why?)}$$

In addition, if $\mathbf{F}$ results in n consecutive displacements represented by $\mathbf{S}_1, \mathbf{S}_2, \ldots, \mathbf{S}_n$, then

$$\mathbf{F} \cdot \mathbf{S} = \mathbf{F} \cdot \mathbf{S}_1 + \mathbf{F} \cdot \mathbf{S}_2 + \cdots + \mathbf{F} \cdot \mathbf{S}_n. \quad \text{(Why?)}$$

analytic geometry

15. OUR POINT OF VIEW

The reader should note that the definitions of addition, subtraction, and inner product of vectors *were not* made in terms of coordinates. At the outset we treated vectors in a *coordinate-free* fashion. (When such is the case, it is often stated that the concepts are "independent of a coordinate system.") And yet, many applications—particularly to geometry—were possible. As we proceeded in our development, new techniques were employed; it is in this light that one should view coordinate systems. That is, coordinate systems should be looked upon as another instrument rather than as another branch of mathematical study. The philosophy that the author is suggesting takes the following form.

The branch of mathematics that we call geometry deals with, among other things, the properties of lines, planes, circles, and spheres. The solutions to problems in this field may be reached by various approaches, some being more natural or stronger than others—depending on the problem at hand. The first approach learned is usually the synthetic method, which has some approximation to that exhibited in Euclid's *Elements*. The present work is devoted to a study of the vector and analytic approach. Hence given a geometric problem, one could give it a vector interpretation, or one could *impose a coordinate system on the problem* and use analytic techniques. Of course, any combination of the three methods is also possible.

In summary, *coordinate systems should not be viewed as intrinsic to geometry but, rather, as another (very powerful) mathematical tool with which one attacks geometric problems.*

Combining our notions of vectors—particularly those of the scalar product—with those of coordinate systems, we shall develop some of the elements of analytic geometry.

16. THE STRAIGHT LINE

We begin with the problem of finding the equation of a straight line in the plane. More precisely, if $P = (x, y)$ is an arbitrary point on a given line $\mathcal{L}$, we seek a mathematical relation that distinguishes $P = (x, y)$ from those points in the plane that are not on $\mathcal{L}$.

There are, of course, many ways to specify a unique line. We begin by specifying two points $P_1(x_1, y_1)$ and $P_2(x_2, y_2)$,[1] and seek the equation of the line determined by these points. The aim is to arrive at an equation in terms of the coordinates of the specified points.

Since P, P_1, and P_2 are all one line (see Figure 48), we may employ Theorem 4 to write

$$\overrightarrow{OP} = (1 - t)\overrightarrow{OP}_1 + t\overrightarrow{OP}_2.$$

[1] This appears to be the most natural way to specify a unique line. It was, in fact, included as Euclid's first axiom, which, freely translated, states that one and only one line can be drawn joining two points.

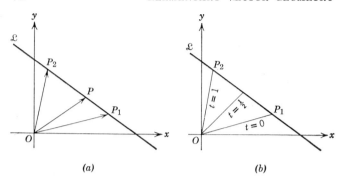

FIGURE 48

Or, in accordance with our convention of designating vectors with a common origin by their endpoints alone, we rewrite this equation in terms of the position vectors of the points

$$\mathbf{P} = (1 - t)\mathbf{P}_1 + t\mathbf{P}_2. \tag{39}$$

Equation 39 is often referred to as a vector equation of line P_1P_2. As t takes on different real number values, we get different vectors for $\mathbf{P}$. For example, if $t = \frac{1}{2}$,

$$\mathbf{P} = (1 - \tfrac{1}{2})\mathbf{P}_1 + \tfrac{1}{2}\mathbf{P}_2 = \tfrac{1}{2}\mathbf{P}_1 + \tfrac{1}{2}\mathbf{P}_2$$

is the position vector of the midpoint of segment P_1P_2.

The auxiliary variable t is called a *parameter* and (39) is also referred to as a *parametric (vector) representation* of line $\mathcal{L}$.

Rewriting (39) in terms of the basis vectors, we have

$$x\mathbf{i} + y\mathbf{j} = (1 - t)x_1\mathbf{i} + (1 - t)y_1\mathbf{j} + tx_2\mathbf{i} + ty_2\mathbf{j}$$
$$= [x_1 + t(x_2 - x_1)]\mathbf{i} + [y_1 + t(y_2 - y_1)]\mathbf{j}.$$

However, the representation of a vector in terms of basis

vectors is unique.   Therefore

$$\begin{cases} x = x_1 + t(x_2 - x_1) \\ y = y_1 + t(y_2 - y_1) \end{cases} \tag{40}$$

are the parametric equations of line $\mathcal{L}$ in *analytic* or *coordinate* (in contrast to vector) *form.*

EXAMPLE 16. Find parametric representations of (*a*) the x-axis and (*b*) the line joining $(3, 1)$ and $(-2, 3)$.

(*a*) The reader knows, of course, that the equation of the x-axis is $y = 0$, but we shall now attempt to verify that this is the case by using (40). Taking two points, say $(0, 0)$ and $(0, 1)$, on the x-axis, we write

$$\begin{cases} x = 0 + t(1 - 0) \\ y = 0 + t(0 - 0). \end{cases}$$

Thus the parametric equations of the x-axis are

$$\begin{cases} x = t \\ y = 0. \end{cases}$$

No matter what the value of t, the y-coordinate is always zero. Therefore $y = 0$ is a sufficient description of the line.

(*b*) Calling $P_1 = (3, 1)$ and $P_2 = (-2, 3)$, and applying (40), yields

$$\begin{cases} x = 3 + t(-2 - 3) \\ y = 1 + t(3 - 1). \end{cases}$$

In simplified form:

$$x = 3 - 5t$$
$$y = 1 + 2t.$$

If, instead, we had begun with $P_1 = (-2, 3)$ and $P_2 = (3, 1)$, (40) would yield:

$$\begin{cases} x = -2 + 5t \\ y = 3 - 2t, \end{cases}$$

a different parametric representation of the same line. Thus we see that *the parametric representation of a line is not unique.*

It depends on the choice of points used to derive the parametric equations.

In many instances it is desirable to eliminate the parameter and to write a line in some form without an auxiliary variable. In order to accomplish such elimination we rewrite (40) as

$$x - x_1 = t(x_2 - x_1)$$

$$y - y_1 = t(y_2 - y_1).$$

and divide the second equation by the first, getting

$$\frac{y - y_1}{x - x_1} = \frac{y_2 - y_1}{x_2 - x_1}, \tag{41}$$

which is the equation of the line,[2] in terms of the coordinates of P_1 and P_2 alone. For this reason (41) is called the *two-point form for the equation of a line*. This form states that the ratio of the difference in the y-coordinates to the difference of the x-coordinates (taken in the same order) of any two points on the line is the same, namely $\frac{y_2 - y_1}{x_2 - x_1}$ (see Figure 49). Note that this is equivalent to the statement that all the triangles in Figure 49 are similar. It should also be noted that this ratio, $\frac{y_2 - y_1}{x_2 - x_1}$, is precisely the ratio of the coefficients of t in the parametric form of the line. Thus at least one feature of the parametric form is independent of the points used to

---

[2] Strictly speaking, (41) is not the equation of the line, for it is not satisfied by (x_1, y_1). The equation satisfied by all points of the line is $y - y_1 = \frac{y_2 - y_1}{x_2 - x_1} (x - x_1)$, while (41) describes this line with the point (x_1, y_1) deleted. We choose to use (41), in spite of the slight inaccuracy, because of its easily remembered symmetric form.

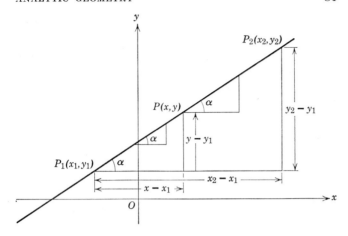

FIGURE 49

derive the equations.   (See Example 16b where $\frac{2}{-5}$ is the ratio of the coefficients of t.)

Since the ratio $\dfrac{y_2 - y_1}{x_2 - x_1}$ is so intrinsic to the algebraic representation of the line, we discuss it further in the light of it being the tangent of the angle labeled α in Figure 49.   We proceed by first giving angle α a name, *the angle of inclination of line* $\mathcal{L}$.   *The angle of inclination of a line* is the angle formed by the given line and the positive x-axis.   That is, α is measured counterclockwise from the positive side of the x-axis to the portion of line $\mathcal{L}$ that lies above the x-axis.   If $\mathcal{L}$ is parallel to the x-axis, we say that the angle of inclination of $\mathcal{L}$ is zero. The tangent of the angle of inclination is termed the *slope* of the line.   Thus

$$\text{slope of } \mathcal{L} = \tan \alpha = \frac{y_2 - y_1}{x_2 - x_1}. \qquad (42)$$

Consequently, (42) states the formula for the slope of a line in terms of two given points; and (41) says, in effect, that any two points used in the computation yield the very same slope.

A difficulty occurs when $x_2 - x_1 = 0$; then the division that produced (41) is not legitimate, for dividing by zero is undefined in arithmetic. Analyzing this case separately (see Figure 50), we see that the line must be vertical in order that $x_1 = x_2$. The angle of inclination is $\pi/2$. The reader is undoubtedly familiar with the fact that the tangent of $\pi/2$ is undefined; i.e. there is no real number that equals $\tan \pi/2$. Thus vertical lines have no slopes; the concept is merely undefined for such lines. However, if $\alpha \neq \pi/2$ and $0 \leq \alpha < \pi$, then $\tan \alpha$ is defined, hence *vertical lines are the only ones that have no slope.*

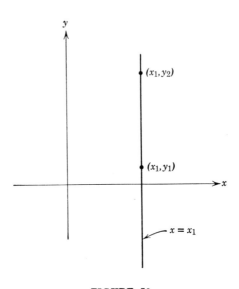

FIGURE 50

The equation of the vertical line under discussion is $x = x_1$ which, if confusing to the reader, should be thought of as stating: for every value of y, x is always equal to x_1. Vertical lines all have the form

$$x = \text{constant};$$

and the reader can easily show that horizontal lines all have the form

$$y = \text{constant}.$$

Continuing our analysis of the equation of the straight line, we solve equation 41 for y:

$$y = \frac{y_2 - y_1}{x_2 - x_1}\, x + \frac{y_2 - y_1}{x_2 - x_1}\, x_1 + y_1.$$

Simplifying this expression by making the replacements

$$m = \frac{y_2 - y_1}{x_2 - x_1} \qquad \text{and} \qquad b = \frac{y_2 - y_1}{x_2 - x_1}\, x_1 + y_1,$$

we get

$$y = mx + b \tag{43}$$

as the equation of the line. Note that m, the coefficient of x, is the slope of the line. Is there a geometric interpretation of the constant b? The answer is easily determined by observing the $y = b$ when $x = 0$. Thus the point $(0, b)$ is on the line. This is the point at which the line (43) crosses or intercepts the y-axis, and it is therefore called the y-intercept. Equation 43 is termed the *slope-intercept form* for the equation of a line, for, from this equation we can immediately read off the slope m and the y-intercept, $(0, b)$ of the line.

EXAMPLE 17. We return to the line (of the last example) determined by $P_1 = (3, 1)$ and $P_2 = (-2, 3)$ and ask several pertinent questions regarding it.

(1) What is its equation in two-point form?

By (41) we have

$$\frac{y-1}{x-3} = \frac{3-1}{-2-3}$$

or

$$\frac{y-1}{x-3} = -\frac{2}{5}. \quad \left(\text{Observe that its slope is } \frac{-2}{5}.\right)$$

(2) What is the equation of the line in slope-intercept form? Solving for y, we get $y = -\frac{2}{5}x + \frac{11}{5}$, so that $m = -\frac{2}{5}$ and $b = \frac{11}{5}$.

(3) We graph the line (Figure 51).   A simple procedure that applies the slope-intercept form is first to locate the y-intercept $(0, \frac{11}{5})$ as one point of the graph.   Then, making use of the slope idea, we proceed five units to the right and two units downward to locate a second point of the graph.

(4) What is the x-intercept?

In the process of answering this rather simple question we shall digress a bit and reflect on the nature of "the equation of the line."   Logically, the equation $y = -\frac{2}{5}x + \frac{11}{5}$ is a sentence, which is true for only certain choices of x and y.   That is, some ordered pairs (x, y) render the sentence true; these pairs are the coordinates of points that are said to lie on the line $y = -\frac{2}{5}x + \frac{11}{5}$.   All the ordered pairs that render the statement false represent points not on the line $y = -\frac{2}{5}x + \frac{11}{5}$. We therefore check to see whether a given point, say $(3, 1)$,

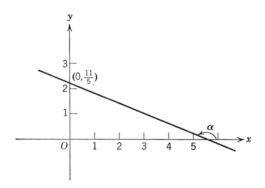

FIGURE 51

is on the line by substituting the coordinates in the sentence and determining whether the sentence is rendered true. Here we have $1 = -\frac{2}{5}(3) + \frac{11}{5}$, which is true. Hence $(3, 1)$ is actually on the line.

In the language of set theory it would be said that a line is a set of points that, expressed analytically, is a set of ordered pairs. Thus a line $\mathfrak{L}$, whose slope is m and whose y-intercept is $(0, b)$, is defined by the statement:

$$\mathfrak{L} = \{(x, y)|y = mx + b\}.$$

The line in Example 17 is then the following set:

$$\{(x, y)|y = -\frac{2}{5}x + \frac{11}{5}\}.$$

Continuing the line of reasoning, we consider the problem of finding the point of intersection of two lines, $\mathfrak{L}_1$ and $\mathfrak{L}_2$, where

$$\begin{aligned}
\mathfrak{L}_1: y &= m_1 x + b_1 \\
\mathfrak{L}_2: y &= m_2 x + b_2.
\end{aligned} \tag{44}$$

The point of intersection (there is, at most, one unless $\mathfrak{L}_1 = \mathfrak{L}_2$) is the ordered pair rendering both statements $\mathfrak{L}_1$ and $\mathfrak{L}_2$ true, simultaneously.[3] That is, we seek the ordered pair that satisfies both equations simultaneously. Finding the pair, if it exists, is then a matter of elementary algebra—solving for the solution to a set of two simultaneous linear equations.

Thus finding the x-intercept of our line is the problem of solving for the solution of the pair of equations:

$$\begin{aligned}
y &= -\frac{2}{5}x + \frac{11}{5} \\
y &= 0 \quad (x \text{ axis}).
\end{aligned}$$

The x-intercept is therefore $(\frac{11}{2}, 0)$.

---

[3] The use of the symbols $\mathfrak{L}_1$ and $\mathfrak{L}_2$ to mean both *lines and sentences* in one paragraph might be frowned upon by some logicians, but this economy of symbols should not cause the reader any confusion. In the rigorous axiomatic treatment of analytic geometry a straight line may be defined as a set whose defining sentence is of the form $ax + by + c = 0$ (see equation (49)). This definition includes vertical lines as well as those that have slope defined.

A Euclidean theorem states: If two lines are cut by a transversal so that a pair of corresponding angles are equal, the two lines are parallel; and conversely, if two parallel lines are cut by a transversal, corresponding angles are equal. Applying this to our treatment of analytic geometry, we may say that *two lines are parallel if and only if they possess the same angle of inclination.* For nonvertical lines, it may be stated that *two lines are parallel if and only if they have the same slope.*

EXAMPLE 18. To find the equation of the line parallel to $y = -\frac{2}{5}x + \frac{11}{5}$ and passing through $(10, -2)$.

Since the line we seek must have slope $m = -\frac{2}{5}$, we may write it in the form

$$y = -\tfrac{2}{5}x + b, \tag{45}$$

with b remaining to be determined. In accordance with the foregoing discussion, the substitution of $(10, -2)$ in (45) should render it true. Thus $-2 = -\frac{2}{5}(10) + b$. Consequently, $b = 2$, and the equation is completely determined: $y = -\frac{2}{5}x + 2$. (For another approach, see (equation 46) in Exercise 8 below.)

EXERCISES

1. Derive the equation of the line determined by $(5, 4)$ and $(3, 1)$ in:
    (a) the vector form as expressed in (39);
    (b) Parametric form;
    (c) two-point form.

2. (a) What is the slope of the line determined in Exercise 1?
    (b) What are its x- and y-intercepts?

3. Derive the equation of the line:
    (a) through $(-5, 4)$ and having y-intercept -5; that is, through $(0, -5)$.
    (b) whose slope is 2 and x-intercept is -3.
    (c) parallel to $2x - y = 3$ and through $(1, 1)$.

4. What is the point of intersection of the line whose equation is $2x - 3y = 12$ and the line whose equation is $2x - 5y = 12$?

5. Sketch (a) $2x - 3y = 12$.
   (b) $2x - 5y = 12$.
   (c) $3y + 7 = 0$.
   (d) $y - 2x = 1$.
   (e) $y = 4$.
   (f) $x = \pi$.
   (g) $\begin{cases} x = 2 - 2t \\ y = -1 + t \end{cases}$
   (h) $\begin{cases} x = t \\ y = 1 - t. \end{cases}$

6. (a) Find the point of intersection of the medians of the triangle determined by $A = (-2, 1)$, $B = (5, -2)$, and $C = (3, -2)$.   (Don't use the equations of the medians!)

   (b) What is the equation of the median emanating from B?

   (c) Find the equation of the interior angle bisector at A. (*Hint.* A vector emanating from A, which bisects angle A,

is $\mathbf{V} = \dfrac{\overrightarrow{AB}}{|\overrightarrow{AB}|} + \dfrac{\overrightarrow{AC}}{|\overrightarrow{AC}|}$.

7. (a) Find the equation of the line with an inclination of $\pi/6$ and passing through $(1, -2)$.

   (b) What is the equation of the line through $(1, -2)$ whose slope is undefined?

   (c) What is the equation of the line through $(1, -2)$ whose slope is zero?

8. (a) The equation for the line through (x_1, y_1), with slope m, is given by

$$\frac{y - y_1}{x - x_1} = m. \quad (\textit{point-slope form}) \qquad (46)$$

Justify (46).   (See footnote 2, page 80.)

   (b) The equation for the line with x-intercept of $(0, a)$ and y-intercept of $(0, b)$ is given by

$$\frac{x}{a} + \frac{y}{b} = 1. \quad (\textit{intercept-form}) \qquad (47)$$

Justify (47).

9. Booby traps:

(a) Sketch $x + y = x + y$.

(b) Sketch $\begin{cases} x = 1 \\ y = t. \end{cases}$

(c) Find an equation for a line whose inclination is $\pi/2$ and whose x-intercept is 0.

17. ANALYTIC GEOMETRY OF THE LINE CONTINUED

Returning to the use of vectors, we pose the question: What is the equation of the line $\mathcal{L}$ through the fixed point $P_0 = (x_0, y_0)$ and perpendicular to the vector $\mathbf{N} = a\mathbf{i} + b\mathbf{j}$?

If $P = (x, y)$ is the general point of the line $\mathcal{L}$ (see Figure 52), we know that $\overrightarrow{P_0P} \perp \mathbf{N}$ or $\overrightarrow{P_0P} \cdot \mathbf{N} = 0$. Therefore

$$[(x - x_0)\mathbf{i} + (y - y_0)\mathbf{j}] \cdot (a\mathbf{i} + b\mathbf{j}) = 0$$

or

$$a(x - x_0) + b(y - y_0) = 0, \tag{48}$$

which is the equation of line $\mathcal{L}$. We can rewrite (48) as

$$ax + by - (ax_0 + by_0) = 0$$

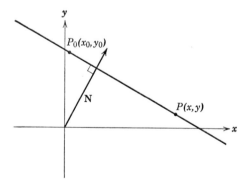

FIGURE 52

or, more simply, as

$$ax + by + c = 0, \qquad \text{where } c = -(ax_0 + by_0), \quad (49)$$

which is the general equation for a straight line in the (x, y)-plane. Equation 49 can be solved for y (provided $b \neq 0$), in which case we will have the line in slope-intercept form. In the event that $b = 0$, (49) yields the vertical line $x = -c/a$ (a and b cannot both be zero, for then (49) would become the trivial sentence $0 = 0$, which is true for all points in the plane). Thus (49) includes all possible straight lines, vertical and nonvertical.

If the concept of slope is carried over to vectors, we find that the slope of **N** is b/a (if $a \neq 0$) and the slope of (49), which can be found from its slope-intercept form $y = -(a/b)x - c/a$, is $-a/b$. We therefore conclude that:

two lines (neither of them vertical) are perpendicular if and only if their slopes are negative reciprocals of one another.

That is, if m_1 is the slope of line $\mathfrak{L}_1$, and m_2 the slope of line $\mathfrak{L}_2$,

$$\mathfrak{L}_1 \perp \mathfrak{L}_2 \qquad \text{if and only if} \qquad m_1 = -\frac{1}{m_2}.$$

(It should be observed that there are two parts to this result but only one has been justified here. The reader should therefore complete the justification.)

If $\mathfrak{L}_1 \perp \mathfrak{L}_2$ and $\mathfrak{L}_1$ is vertical (no slope), then $\mathfrak{L}_2$ must be horizontal, i.e., $m_2 = 0$.

EXAMPLE 19. Find the equation of the line through $(2, -1)$ and perpendicular to the vector $3\mathbf{i} - 4\mathbf{j}$.

Following the scheme of reasoning that climaxed with (48), we write

$$[(x - 2)\mathbf{i} + (y - (-1))\mathbf{j}] \cdot (3\mathbf{i} - 4\mathbf{j}) = 0;$$

or

$$3(x - 2) - 4(y + 1) = 0,$$

which, simplified and put in the form of (49), reads:

$$3x - 4y - 10 = 0.$$

EXAMPLE 20. Find the equation of the line through $(2, -1)$ and perpendicular to $3x - 4y - 10 = 0$.

Writing the given line in slope-intercept form

$$y = \tfrac{3}{4}x - \tfrac{5}{2},$$

we see that its slope is $\tfrac{3}{4}$. Therefore the slope of the desired line is $-1/\tfrac{3}{4} = -\tfrac{4}{3}$. (Check this with slope of **N** in Example 19.) Therefore, by using the point-slope form (46), the line we seek can be written

$$\frac{y - (-1)}{x - 2} = -\frac{4}{3}, \qquad \text{or} \qquad 4x - 3y - 5 = 0.$$

EXERCISES

1. If a line $\mathcal{L}$ is given by $ax + by + c = 0$, find an expression for a vector **N** perpendicular to $\mathcal{L}$, in terms of the coefficients in the equation of $\mathcal{L}$.

2. Find the equation of the line perpendicular to $2x - y - 1 = 0$ and through the origin.

3. Find the equation of the perpendicular bisector of the segment joining $(1, -3)$ and $(3, 5)$.

4. Find two vectors of unit length perpendicular to $2x - y - 1 = 0$.

18. DISTANCE FROM A POINT TO A LINE

The problem of determining the (minimum) distance between a point $P_0 = (x_0, y_0)$ and a line

$$\mathcal{L}: ax + by + c = 0$$

is easily handled by vectors. We shall actually derive a formula for this distance, but it is the author's suggestion that the reader not memorize this formula. One of the strong advantages of thinking in terms of vectors—as opposed to pure analytics—is that fewer formulas need to be remembered. A thorough familiarity with the

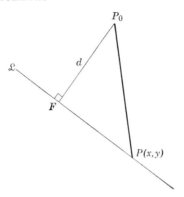

FIGURE 53

basic vector tools often enables one to solve problems by following a basic pattern of reasoning from first principles—just as easily as applying a complicated formula. The present problem is a case in point.

Let $P = (x, y)$ be a general point on $\mathcal{L}$. Then the minimum distance d from P_0 to $\mathcal{L}$ could be thought of as the magnitude of the projection of $\overrightarrow{PP_0}$ on the perpendicular $\overrightarrow{PF}$ to $\mathcal{L}$ (see Figure 53). Thus the dot product will serve as an aid to finding d. Using the result of the last section, we write a vector perpendicular to $\mathcal{L}$ as $\mathbf{N} = a\mathbf{i} + b\mathbf{j}$. Applying Theorem 6, we have

$$d = \left|\mathrm{pr}_{\mathbf{N}}\overrightarrow{PP_0}\right| = \frac{\left|\overrightarrow{PP_0} \cdot \mathbf{N}\right|}{|\mathbf{N}|}$$

$$= \left|[(x - x_0)\mathbf{i} + (y - y_0)\mathbf{j}] \cdot \frac{a\mathbf{i} + b\mathbf{j}}{\sqrt{a^2 + b^2}}\right|$$

$$= \frac{\left|ax_0 + by_0 - ax - by\right|}{\sqrt{a^2 + b^2}}.$$

But, $-ax - by = c$, so we finally have

$$d = \frac{|ax_0 + by_0 + c|}{\sqrt{a^2 + b^2}}, \tag{50}$$

which is a formula for the distance d in terms of the coordinates of the given point P_0 and the constants in the given line $\mathfrak{L}$.

EXAMPLE 21. Find the distance from $P_0 = (1, 3)$ to the line $\mathfrak{L}: y = \frac{1}{2}x - 1$.

Although formula (50) for the distance has been derived in this very section, we shall illustrate the point of the suggestion made above by abandoning the use of (50) in favor of working from first principles.

We begin by writing $\mathfrak{L}$ in the form $x - 2y - 2 = 0$, so that a vector perpendicular to $\mathfrak{L}$ can immediately be written as $\mathbf{i} - 2\mathbf{j}$. In the computation used in arriving at d, the reader doubtlessly observed that we were forced to divide by $|\mathbf{N}|$, which meant that we were actually computing the projection by projecting on the unit vector $\dfrac{\mathbf{N}}{|\mathbf{N}|}$. It might, therefore, be more convenient if we convert the perpendicular vector

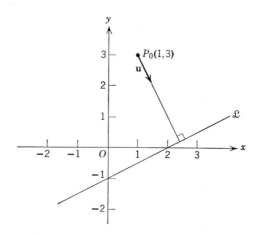

FIGURE 54

to a unit vector at the outset of our present computation. Such a unit vector is

$$\mathbf{U} = \frac{\mathbf{i} - 2\mathbf{j}}{\sqrt{5}}.$$

The distance d is then the magnitude of the projection of $\overrightarrow{P_0P_1}$ on $\mathbf{U}$, where P_1 is any point on $\mathcal{L}$. A rather simple choice for P_1 is the y-intercept of $\mathcal{L}$, namely $(0, -1)$. Hence,

$$d = |\overrightarrow{P_0P_1} \cdot \mathbf{U}| = |\,(\mathrm{pr_U}\,\overrightarrow{P_0P_1})|\mathbf{U}|\,| = |\mathrm{pr_U}\,\overrightarrow{P_0P_1}|$$

$$= \left| [(0 - 1)\mathbf{i} + (-1 - 3)\mathbf{j}] \cdot \frac{\mathbf{i} - 2\mathbf{j}}{\sqrt{5}} \right|$$

$$= \left| (-\mathbf{i} - 4\mathbf{j}) \cdot \frac{\mathbf{i} - 2\mathbf{j}}{\sqrt{5}} \right| = \frac{|-1 + 8|}{\sqrt{5}}$$

$$= \frac{7\sqrt{5}}{5}.$$

Any other choice of P_1, say $P_1 = (2, 0)$, should give the same result:

$$d = \left| [(2 - 1)\mathbf{i} + (0 - 3)\mathbf{j}] \cdot \frac{\mathbf{i} - 2\mathbf{j}}{\sqrt{5}} \right|$$

$$= \left| \frac{1 + 6}{\sqrt{5}} \right| = \frac{7\sqrt{5}}{5}.$$

Even a general point $P_1 = (x_1, y_1)$ of $\mathcal{L}$ would yield the explicit computation:

$$d = \left| [(x_1 - 1)\mathbf{i} + (y_1 - 3)\mathbf{j}] \cdot \frac{\mathbf{i} - 2\mathbf{j}}{\sqrt{5}} \right|$$

$$= \frac{|x_1 - 2y_1 + 5|}{\sqrt{5}}.$$

But, since (x_1, y_1) is on $\mathcal{L}$, we know that $x_1 - 2y_1 = 2$. Therefore

$$d = \frac{|2 + 5|}{\sqrt{5}} = \frac{7}{\sqrt{5}} = \frac{7\sqrt{5}}{5}.$$

Suppose we had begun with $\mathbf{U} = \dfrac{-\mathbf{i} + 2\mathbf{j}}{\sqrt{5}}$ as the unit vector perpendicular to $\mathcal{L}$. Then the sign of the projection would be changed; but since we are taking the magnitude, or absolute value of the projection, the value for d would be the same as in our previous computations.

As soon as the method of projection is grasped, the computations can be made simply and directly, without any reference to a formula. However, a thorough understanding of vector thinking comes only with the practice of such thinking. And it is precisely to promote such practice that exercises are included. Be sure to do a good share of them!

EXERCISES

1. Find the distance from $(1, 2)$ to $x - 2y = 5$.

2. Find the distance from $(1, -2)$ to $x - 2y = 5$.

3. Find the distance from $(1, -2)$ to $-x + 2y + 5 = 0$.

4. Find the magnitude of the projection of the segment AB on the line $x - 2y = 5$, where $A = (1, 1)$ and $B = (2, -1)$.

5. Find the magnitude of the projection of segment AB on the vector $3\mathbf{i} - 4\mathbf{j}$ where A and B are the same as in 4.

19. ANALYTIC METHOD OF PROOF

In accordance with the philosophy described in Section 15, we shall now illustrate the application of analytic methods to proving results of geometry. The spirit of these illustrations will be to divorce our work from the ideas of synthetic geometry (e.g., congruence, similarity) in favor of working with coordinates, slope, and other notions that are analytic in character.

EXAMPLE 22. Prove that the line joining the midpoints of two sides of a triangle is parallel to the third side and equal to one half of it.

Again, in accordance with the philosophy put forth in Section 15, we view this as a geometry problem and impose a

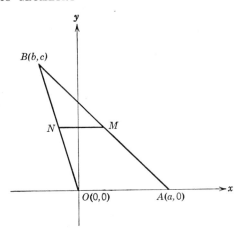

FIGURE 55

coordinate system upon it. We therefore impose the coordinate system in such a manner as to facilitate our work. For example, we may choose the origin as one vertex of the triangle and the x-axis to be along one side of the triangle (see Figure 55). If we do this, and if we desire our proof to hold for all triangles, there is no further choice available. Calling the triangle OAB, we assign coordinates as follows:

$$O = (0, 0), \quad A = (a, 0), \quad B = (b, c).$$

Next, we compute the coordinates of M, the midpoint of AB, and N, the midpoint of OB, by means of the formula derived in Example 10d.

$$M = \left(\frac{a + b}{2}, \frac{c}{2}\right) \quad \text{and} \quad N = \left(\frac{b}{2}, \frac{c}{2}\right).$$

The slope of $MN = \dfrac{c/2 - c/2}{b/2 - (a + b)/2} = 0$, which proves that

MN is parallel to OA.

As for the second part of the result, we compute the length of segment MN.

$$|MN| = \sqrt{\left(\frac{c}{2} - \frac{c}{2}\right)^2 + \left(\frac{b}{2} - \frac{a+b}{2}\right)^2} = \sqrt{\frac{a^2}{4}} = \frac{|a|}{2},$$

which shows that $|MN| = \frac{1}{2}|AO|$.

EXAMPLE 23. Prove that the diagonals of a parallelogram bisect each other.

Again we elect to place the coordinate axes in a convenient position. Let the parallelogram be $OABC$, where $O = (0, 0)$, $A = (a, 0)$, and $C = (b, c)$, as noted in Figure 56. If we ascribe coordinates, say (d, e), to point B, we find that d and e are dependent on the coordinates chosen for the other three vertices of the parallelogram. That is, the condition that the figure is a parallelogram, namely, that its opposite sides are parallel, forces certain coordinates upon B.

Since CB is parallel to OA, the slope of CB is zero; that is, $(e - c)/(d - b) = 0$, which implies that $e = c$. And, since OC is parallel to AB, $(c - 0)/(b - 0) = (c - 0)/(d - a)$; or $d = a + b$. Thus, $B = (a + b, c)$.

Now that we have imposed the parallelogram condition, we are free to attack our problem—finding the mid-points of the diagonals. The midpoint of $OB = ((a + b)/2, \ c/2)$ and the midpoint of $AC = ((a + b)/2, c/2)$, which establishes the result.

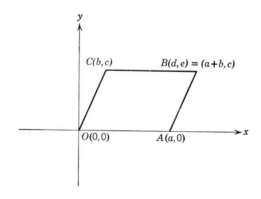

FIGURE 56

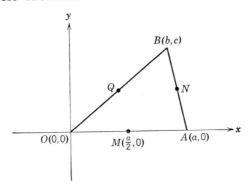

FIGURE 57

EXAMPLE 24. Prove analytically that the medians of a triangle meet in a point.

Let the triangle be OAB, as shown in Figure 57, where $O = (0, 0)$, $A = (a, 0)$ and $B = (b, c)$. Call M the midpoint of OA, N the midpoint of AB, and Q the midpoint of OB.

Then $M = \left(\dfrac{a}{2}, 0\right)$, $N = \left(\dfrac{a + b}{2}, \dfrac{c}{2}\right)$ and $Q = \left(\dfrac{b}{2}, \dfrac{c}{2}\right)$.

The equations of the median lines are found to be:

ON: $y = \dfrac{c}{a + b} x$

BM: $y = \dfrac{c}{b - (a/2)} \left(x - \dfrac{a}{2}\right)$ or $y = \dfrac{2cx}{2b - a} - \dfrac{ac}{2b - a}$

AQ: $y = \dfrac{c/2}{b/2 - a} (x - a)$ or $y = \dfrac{c}{b - 2a} (x - a)$.

For the point of intersection of ON and BM, we solve the first two equations as a simultaneous pair, getting

$$x = \frac{a + b}{3} \quad \text{and} \quad y = \frac{c}{3}.$$

For the point of intersection of ON and AQ, we solve the first and third equations simultaneously, arriving at the same point $((a + b)/3, c/3)$. Thus, the medians of triangle OAB all meet at $((a + b)/3, c/3)$.

For the purposes of further illustration, we use the vector approach to check the coordinates of the point P of intersection of the medians. Referring to Example 10e, the position vector of P is written

$$\mathbf{P} = \tfrac{1}{3}\mathbf{O} + \tfrac{1}{3}\mathbf{A} + \tfrac{1}{3}\mathbf{B}$$

$$= \tfrac{1}{3}(0\mathbf{i} + 0\mathbf{j}) + \tfrac{1}{3}(a\mathbf{i}) + \tfrac{1}{3}(b\mathbf{i} + c\mathbf{j})$$

$$= \tfrac{1}{3}(a + b)\mathbf{i} + \frac{c}{3}\,\mathbf{j}$$

Thus $P = ((a + b)/3, c/3)$, which checks with the above computation.

It seems clear that the median problem is more easily handled by use of vectors than by pure analytics.

EXERCISES

1. Prove: In any triangle the sum of the squares of the medians is equal to three-fourths the sum of the squares of the three sides.

2. Prove: The sum of the squares of two sides of a triangle is equal to one-half the square of the third side, increased by twice the square of the median on that side.

3. Prove: The sum of the squares of the four sides of a parallelogram is equal to the sum of the squares of the diagonals. (Compare with vector proof.)

4. Prove: The sum of the squares of the four sides of any quadrilateral is equal to the sum of the squares of the diagonals increased by four times the square of the line joining the midpoints of the diagonals.

5. Prove analytically:
   (a) the median of a trapezoid is parallel to the bases;
   (b) the lines joining the midpoints of the sides of a quadrilateral form a parallelogram;

(c) in any quadrilateral, the segments joining the midpoints of opposite sides intersect in a point that is the midpoint of the segment joining the midpoints of the diagonals.

6. If line $\mathcal{L}_1$ has a slope of m_1 and an angle of inclination θ_1, and if line $\mathcal{L}_2$ has a slope of m_2 and angle of inclination θ_2, use the formula for $\tan(\theta_2 - \theta_1)$ to determine $\tan \theta$, where θ is the angle between $\mathcal{L}_1$ and $\mathcal{L}_2$ (measuring counterclockwise from $\mathcal{L}_1$ to $\mathcal{L}_2$). See Figure 58.

7. Discuss the difficulty of using the result of Exercise 6 when the lines $\mathcal{L}_1$ and $\mathcal{L}_2$ are perpendicular.

8. Find the angles of the triangles
   (a) (5, 0), (8, 4), (−4, 13).
   (b) (2, 6), (6, 0), (−3, 8).

9. The slopes of two lines are given as −2 and 3. Find the slopes of the lines that bisect the angles between them.

10. If $O = (0, 0)$, $A = (\sqrt{3}, 1)$, and $B = (2\sqrt{3}, 1)$, find the equation of the line bisecting angle AOB.

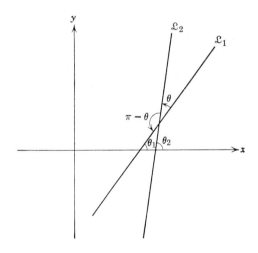

FIGURE 58

11. If $\mathcal{L}_1$ is given by $a_1x + b_1y + c_1 = 0$ and $\mathcal{L}_2$ is given by $a_1x + b_1y + c_1 = 0$, we define a *linear combination* of $\mathcal{L}_1$ and $\mathcal{L}_2$ as an equation of the form

$$m(a_1x + b_1y + c_1) + n(a_2x + b_2y + c_2) = 0 \qquad (51)$$

(a) Why is the locus described by a linear combination of two lines also a line, if m and n are not both zero?

(b) If P is the point of intersection of $\mathcal{L}_1$ and $\mathcal{L}_2$, prove that any linear combination of $\mathcal{L}_1$ and $\mathcal{L}_2$ also passes through P; and conversely, every line through P is a linear combination of $\mathcal{L}_1$ and $\mathcal{L}_2$. The consequence of this result is that the set of all lines through P, often called *the pencil of lines with vertex P*, can be written by the single equation 51, where m and n range over all the real numbers (excluding the case $m = n = 0$).

(c) If $\mathcal{L}_1$ is parallel to $\mathcal{L}_2$, prove that any linear combination of them is also parallel to each of $\mathcal{L}_1$ and $\mathcal{L}_2$. In this case (51) represents the set of all lines parallel to $\mathcal{L}_1$ (or $\mathcal{L}_2$), often called a *pencil of parallel lines*.

12. *Using the results of Exercise* 11, find the line through the point of intersection of $x - 2y = 3$ and $4x - 2y = 15$, and passing through the origin, without finding the point of intersection of the given lines. (Be sure to follow (51) carefully!)

13. (a) Write an equation that represents the pencil of lines through $(1, -2)$.

(b) Write an equation that represents the pencil of lines with inclination $\pi/6$.

14. (a) Find the line through the point of intersection of the lines whose equations are $x - 2y + 4 = 0$ and $2x + 3y - 3 = 0$, and through the point $(0, \frac{1}{2})$.

(b) Find the line through the point of intersection of the lines whose equations are $3x + 2y + 8 = 0$ and $x + 8y + 7 = 0$, and through the point $(\frac{3}{7}, 0)$.

15. By using the results of Exercise 11, prove the medians of a triangle meet in a point.

20. CIRCLES

Let $P_0 = (x_0, y_0)$ be the center of a circle of radius r and $P = (x, y)$ a general point of the circle (see Figure

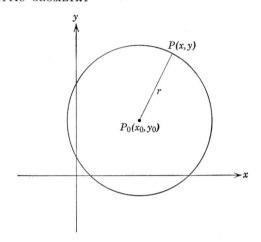

FIGURE 59

59). Then the vector equation of the circle is easily found by imposing the condition that $\left|\overrightarrow{P_0P}\right| = r$. Utilizing the position vectors of the points, we write the vector equation of the circle as

$$\left|\mathbf{P} - \mathbf{P}_0\right| = \left|r \right. \tag{52}$$

or $\sqrt{(\mathbf{P} - \mathbf{P}_0) \cdot (\mathbf{P} - \mathbf{P}_0)} = r$. To get the analytic form, we rewrite (52) as

$$\left|(x - x_0)\mathbf{i} + (y - y_0)\mathbf{j}\right| = r$$

or

$$\sqrt{(x - x_0)^2 + (y - y_0)^2} = r.$$

Finally, by squaring both members, we get

$$(x - x_0)^2 + (y - y_0)^2 = r^2 \tag{53}$$

as the equation of the circle whose center is (x_0, y_0) and whose radius is r.

Concerning the equation of the circle, it should be noted that: (1) It is quadratic in x and y; and (2) it has the coefficients of x^2 and y^2 both equal (to unity), when in the form (53).

Expanding (53), we get

$$x^2 - 2x_0 x + x_0{}^2 + y^2 - 2y_0 y + y_0{}^2 = r^2.$$

By grouping the constant terms and designating coefficients of the variables by a single letter, we may write this equation in the form

$$x^2 + y^2 - Ax + By + C = 0, \qquad (54)$$

which is, of course, the equation of a circle but of such a nature as to obscure its essential characteristics, namely, the radius and center of the circle.

We pose two questions, which can be answered simultaneously. (1) Does every equation of the form (54) represent a circle? (2) If it does represent a circle, how can we find the center and radius?

The answers to both questions depend on whether we can write (54) in the form of (53). We attempt to accomplish this by completing the squares in the parentheses of the expression

$$(x^2 + Ax) + (y^2 + By) = -C.$$

In order to do so we add $A^2/4$ and $B^2/4$ to both members:

$$\left(x^2 + Ax + \frac{A^2}{4}\right) + \left(y^2 + By + \frac{B^2}{4}\right) = \frac{A^2}{4} + \frac{B^2}{4} - C$$

or

$$\left(x + \frac{A}{2}\right)^2 + \left(y + \frac{B}{2}\right)^2 = \frac{A^2}{4} + \frac{B^2}{4} - C,$$

which is in the form of (53), enabling us to say that the center of the circle is $(-A/2, -B/2)$ and the radius is

$\sqrt{A^2/4 + B^2/4 - C}$. The one difficulty that has been overlooked is the question of whether this square root is real or imaginary. If $A^2/4 + B^2/4 - C < 0$, no real circle exists. For example, $x^2 + y^2 = -1$ cannot represent a real locus. However, if $A^2/4 + B^2/4 - C > 0$, we do have a real circle; and if this expression equals zero, the circle degenerates to a point.

EXAMPLE 25. Examine the locus $3x^2 + 3y^2 - 6x + 9y + 2 = 0$.

Since the coefficients of x^2 and y^2 are equal, we may rewrite the equation with these coefficients equal to unity:

$$x^2 + y^2 - 2x + 3y + \frac{2}{3} = 0.$$

Completing the squares, we get

$$(x^2 - 2x + 1) + \left(y^2 + 3y + \frac{9}{4}\right) = 1 + \frac{9}{4} - \frac{2}{3},$$

or

$$(x - 1)^2 + \left(y + \frac{3}{2}\right)^2 = \frac{31}{12}.$$

Hence, the locus is a circle whose center is $(1, -\frac{3}{2})$ and whose radius is $r = \frac{1}{6}\sqrt{93}$.

If we consider a circle of radius r centered at the origin (as in Figure 60), the position vector

$$\mathbf{P} = x\mathbf{i} + y\mathbf{j}$$

can be written in terms of its angle of inclination θ:

$$\mathbf{P} = r \cos \theta \mathbf{i} + r \sin \theta \mathbf{j}.$$

We therefore conclude that

$$\begin{cases} x = r \cos \theta \\ y = r \sin \theta \end{cases} \tag{55}$$

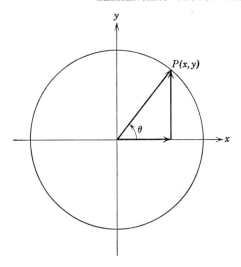

FIGURE 60

are the parametric equations of the given circle where θ is the parameter.

The single equation of the form (53) or (54) that represents a circle of radius r, centered at the origin, may be recovered from (55) by squaring and adding as follows:

$$x^2 = r^2 \cos^2 \theta$$
$$y^2 = r^2 \sin^2 \theta,$$

from which we deduce that

$$x^2 + y^2 = r^2(\cos^2 \theta + \sin^2 \theta).$$

But $\cos^2 \theta + \sin^2 \theta = 1$. Thus

$$x^2 + y^2 = r^2$$

is the equation of the specified circle.

EXERCISES

1. Write the equation of the circle with
   (a) center $(0, 1)$ and radius 2;
   (b) center $(0, -1)$ and radius 2;
   (c) center $(-2, 3)$ and radius 3.

2. Find the equation of the circle
   (a) with center at $(2, -1)$ and passing through the origin;
   (b) passing through $(1, -1)$, $(2, 0)$, and $(0, 3)$;
   (c) having x-intercept 8, y-intercept -12 and passing through the origin.

3. Find the centers and radii of circles having the following equations:
   (a) $x^2 + y^2 - 16x + 12y = 0$;
   (b) $2x^2 - 2y^2 = 9x$;
   (c) $x^2 + y^2 - 10x + 7y + 9 = 0$;
   (d) $3x^2 + 3y^2 + 8x - 4y + 15 = 0$.

4. Find the points of intersection and the equation of the line that contributes the common chord to the circles whose equations are
   (a) $x^2 + y^2 + 8y = 64$
       $x^2 + y^2 - 6x = 16$;
   (b) $x^2 + y^2 + 4x - 25 = 0$
       $x^2 + y^2 - 8y + 3 = 0$. (*Hint.* What is the algebraic meaning of the interesection of loci?)

5. Carry through the following vector approach to determine the equation of the line tangent to a given circle at a given point.

   Let the circle $\mathcal{K}$ be centered at $C = (x_0, y_0)$ and let $Q = (a, b)$ be a point of $\mathcal{K}$. Call $P = (x, y)$ the general point of the line $\mathcal{G}$, which is tangent to $\mathcal{K}$ at (a, b). Using the fact that the radius vector $\overrightarrow{CQ}$ is perpendicular to $\overrightarrow{QP}$, prove that line $\mathcal{G}$ is represented by the equation

   $$(x_0 - a)(x - a) + (y_0 - b)(y - b) = 0.$$

6. Verify the equation for $\mathcal{G}$ given in Exercise 5 by using the point-slope equation of the line and the fact that a radius is perpendicular to the tangent line at the point of contact.

7. Find the equation of the line tangent to
   (a) $x^2 + y^2 + 10x = 60$ at $(4, 2)$;
   (b) $x^2 + y^2 - 12y = 36$ at $(6, 0)$;
   (c) $\left.\begin{array}{l} x = 2\cos\theta \\ y = 2\sin\theta \end{array}\right\}$ at $(\sqrt{2}, \sqrt{2})$;

   (d) $\left.\begin{array}{l} x = 2\cos\theta \\ y = 2\sin\theta \end{array}\right\}$ at $(\sqrt{2}, -\sqrt{2})$.

8. Prove that the parametric equations of a circle with center at (x_0, y_0) and radius r is

$$\begin{cases} x = x_0 + r\cos\theta \\ y = y_0 + r\sin\theta. \end{cases}$$

9. Find a parametric representation of the equation of the circle
   (a) with center $(-1, 2)$ and radius 5;
   (b) $3x^2 + 3y^2 - 6x + 9y - 2 = 0$.

10. Find the points of intersection of the loci whose equations are
   (a) $x^2 + y^2 - 2x - 2y + 1 = 0$ and $x + y = 1$;
   (b) $x^2 + y^2 - 2x - 2y + 1 = 0$ and $x^2 + y^2 = 1$

21. SPHERES

The three-dimensional analogue of the circle is the *sphere*, which may be defined as *the locus of points that are equidistant from a fixed point.* This definition is easily recognized to be precisely that of the circle if the discussion is restricted to a plane. Actually, the very same definition carries over to four-dimensional, five-dimensional, and *n*-dimensional spheres (sometimes called hyperspheres).

Confining our discussion to three dimensions, we call $P_0 = (x_0, y_0, z_0)$ the fixed point (center), $P(x, y, z)$ the general point of the sphere, and r the constant distance (radius of the sphere) between P_0 and P (see Figure 61).

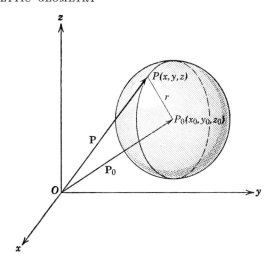

FIGURE 61

Then the vector equation of the sphere, in terms of the position vectors of P_0 and P, is

$$|\mathbf{P} - \mathbf{P}_0| = r \qquad \text{or} \qquad \sqrt{(\mathbf{P} - \mathbf{P}_0) \cdot (\mathbf{P} - \mathbf{P}_0)} = r,$$

precisely the same as (52), which is the vector equation of the circle. In coordinate form we have

$$|(x - x_0)\mathbf{i} + (y - y_0)\mathbf{j} + (z - z_0)\mathbf{k}| = r,$$

or

$$\sqrt{(x - x_0)^2 + (y - y_0)^2 + (z - z_0)^2} = r.$$

Finally, by squaring both members of this last equation, we get

$$(x - x_0)^2 + (y - y_0)^2 + (z - z_0)^2 = r^2$$

as the equation of the sphere whose center is

$$P_0 = (x_0, y_0, z_0)$$

and whose radius is r.

The problem of arriving at a general form for the equation of a sphere (similar to that of (54)) and of converting equations to that form would be quite repetitious of the discussion in Section 20 on circles.   We therefore relegate the details of such a discussion as an exercise for the reader while we now turn attention to other matters relating to the sphere.

The *unit sphere* or *sphere of unit radius*, whose center is at the origin, has the equation

$$x^2 + y^2 + z^2 = 1. \tag{56}$$

We shall analyze the components of the position vector

$$\mathbf{P} = x\mathbf{i} + y\mathbf{j} + z\mathbf{k}$$

of point P on the unit sphere, shown in Figure 62a.

If α is the angle that $\mathbf{P}$ makes with the x-axis, β the angle that $\mathbf{P}$ makes with the y-axis, and γ the angle that $\mathbf{P}$ makes with the z-axis,

$$\mathbf{P} \cdot \mathbf{i} = |\mathbf{P}|\,|\mathbf{i}| \cos \alpha = \cos \alpha$$

and

$$\mathbf{P} \cdot \mathbf{i} = (x\mathbf{i} + y\mathbf{j} + z\mathbf{k}) \cdot \mathbf{i} = x.$$

Therefore $x = \cos \alpha$; similarly, $y = \cos \beta$ and $z = \cos \gamma$. Hence $\mathbf{P} = \cos \alpha\mathbf{i} + \cos \beta\mathbf{j} + \cos \gamma\mathbf{k}$.

Every vector $\mathbf{V}$ (see Figure 62b) in three dimensions is parallel to the position vector of a point P on the unit sphere, so that the direction of $\mathbf{V}$ is completely specified by the angles α, β, and γ associated with the vector $\mathbf{P}$. For this reason we call the angles α, β, and γ the *direction angles* of $\mathbf{V}$ (and also of $\mathbf{P}$), and $\cos \alpha$, $\cos \beta$, and $\cos \gamma$ the *direction cosines* of $\mathbf{V}$ (and of $\mathbf{P}$).

Since $|\mathbf{P}|^2 = \mathbf{P} \cdot \mathbf{P} = 1$, the direction cosines of every vector satisfy the relation

$$\cos^2 \alpha + \cos^2 \beta + \cos^2 \gamma = 1. \tag{57}$$

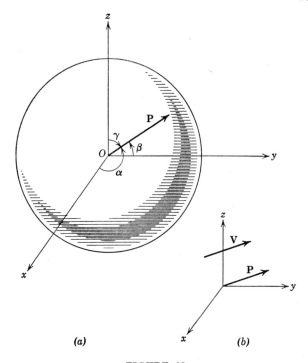

(a)   *(b)*

FIGURE 62

Suppose $\mathbf{V} = l\mathbf{i} + m\mathbf{j} + n\mathbf{k}$. Then the unit vector to which $\mathbf{V}$ is parallel is

$$\frac{\mathbf{V}}{|\mathbf{V}|} = \frac{l\mathbf{i} + m\mathbf{j} + n\mathbf{k}}{\sqrt{l^2 + m^2 + n^2}}.$$

Thus

$$\cos \alpha = \frac{1}{\sqrt{l^2 + m^2 + n^2}}, \quad \cos \beta = \frac{m}{\sqrt{l^2 + m^2 + n^2}},$$

$$\text{(58)}$$

$$\text{and } \cos \gamma = \frac{n}{\sqrt{l^2 + m^2 + n^2}},$$

from which we see that $l:m:n = \cos\alpha:\cos\beta:\cos\gamma$; that is, the numbers l, m, n are proportional to the direction cosines. It is for this reason that l, m, n, are called *direction numbers* of $\mathbf{V}$. We speak of the ordered set $\{l, m, n\}$ as a *set of direction numbers*. Since the direction of $t\mathbf{V} = tl\mathbf{i} + tm\mathbf{j} + tn\mathbf{k}(t \neq 0)$ is the same as that of $\mathbf{V}$ ($t\mathbf{V}$ is parallel to $\mathbf{V}$), we also call $\{tl, tm, tn\}$ (where $t \neq 0$) a set of direction numbers for $\mathbf{V}$. *If some triple of numbers is a set of direction numbers for a given vector, any nonzero multiple of the triple is also a set of direction numbers for the vector*, for both triples designate the same direction (with the possibility of opposite sense) and both triples satisfy the condition of being proportional to the direction cosines.[4]

EXAMPLE 26. Let $\mathbf{V} = 2\mathbf{i} - 3\mathbf{j} + 6\mathbf{k}$.

(a) We give three equivalent sets of direction numbers for $\mathbf{V}$.

From the given representation of $\mathbf{V}$ we see immediately that $\{2, -3, 6\}$ form a set of direction numbers. Two other sets of direction numbers can be found by allowing t to take on two distinct values in the ordered triple $\{2t, -3t, 6t\}$; e.g., $t = -1$ yields $\{-2, 3, -6\}$ and $t = 2$ yields $\{4, -6, 12\}$.

(b) Find the direction cosines of $\mathbf{V}$.

Making use of (58), we write

$$\cos\alpha = \frac{2}{\sqrt{2^2 + (-3)^2 + 6^2}} = \frac{2}{7}, \quad \cos\beta = \frac{-3}{7}, \quad \cos\gamma = \frac{6}{7}.$$

It should be noted that the unit vector

$$\tfrac{1}{7}\mathbf{V} = \tfrac{2}{7}\mathbf{i} - \tfrac{3}{7}\mathbf{j} + \tfrac{6}{7}\mathbf{k},$$

from which the direction cosines can be read off directly, has

---

[4] In some developments, it may be advantageous to have a set of direction numbers for a vector $\mathbf{V}$ actually impart information about the sense of $\mathbf{V}$. If this were the case, we would impose the restriction $t > 0$; for if $t < 0$, then $\{tl, tm, tn\}$ would imply a sense opposite to the original triple $\{l, m, n\}$. However, our development of direction numbers is principally for applications to lines, which, in contrast to vectors, have no sense. Thus, we make the simple restriction that $t \neq 0$.

the same sense of direction as **V**.   However,

$$-\tfrac{1}{7}\mathbf{V} = -\tfrac{2}{7}\mathbf{i} + \tfrac{3}{7}\mathbf{j} - \tfrac{6}{7}\mathbf{k},$$

although oppositely sensed, is also a unit vector and therefore also yields a set of direction cosines $\{-\tfrac{2}{7}, \tfrac{3}{7}, -\tfrac{6}{7}\}$ for the vector **V**.

EXERCISES

1. Find a set of direction cosines for the position vector of the points
   (a) (4, 3, 5),
   (b) (3, −4, 12),
   (c) (0, 0, 1),
   (d) (0, 2, 0).

2. Using the method of Example 25, find the center and radius of the spheres whose equations are
   (a) $4x^2 + 4y^2 + 4z^2 = 8y$,
   (b) $x^2 + y^2 + z^2 + 4x - 6y = 3$.

3. Find the equation of the sphere with
   (a) center at (1, −1, 0) and radius 2,
   (b) center at (−1, 2, −3) and radius $\sqrt{2}$,
   (c) center at the origin and radius 12.

4. Find two sets of direction numbers and two sets of direction cosines for the vector
   (a) $\mathbf{V} = 3\mathbf{i} + \mathbf{j} - \mathbf{k}$.
   (b) $\mathbf{V} = 2\mathbf{i} - \mathbf{j} + \mathbf{k}$.

22. PLANES

The second locus, or surface, that we discuss is the plane, which in some respects is analogous to the line in two dimensions.   Although we have several equivalent choices for a definition, our needs of the moment will best be served by the following:

Definition.   *If P_0 is a fixed point and* **N** *a fixed vector, the locus of points P so that $\overrightarrow{P_0P}$ is perpendicular to* **N** *is called a* plane.   (In Figure 63, we picture **N** positioned so that its origin at P_0.)

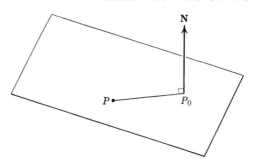

FIGURE 63

An immediate consequence of the definition is that P_0 itself is on the plane, for if $P = P_0$, then $\overrightarrow{P_0P}$ is the zero vector that is perpendicular to $\mathbf{N}$ (see Theorem 5).

Writing the definition in vector language in terms of position vectors, we have

$$(\mathbf{P} - \mathbf{P}_0) \cdot \mathbf{N} = 0, \qquad (59)$$

the vector equation of the plane through P_0 and perpendicular to $\mathbf{N}$.

In order to derive an analytic expression for the plane, we follow the usual procedure of calling the variable point of the plane $P = (x, y, z)$. The fixed elements will be $P_0 = (x_0, y_0, z_0)$ and $\mathbf{N} = a\mathbf{i} + b\mathbf{j} + c\mathbf{k}$. Then (59) becomes

$$[(x - x_0)\mathbf{i} + (y - y_0)\mathbf{j} + (z - z_0)\mathbf{k}] \cdot (a\mathbf{i} + b\mathbf{j} + c\mathbf{k}) = 0.$$

Expanding yields

$$a(x - x_0) + b(y - y_0) + c(z - z_0) = 0, \qquad (60)$$

which is *the analytic equation of the plane through (x_0, y_0, z_0) and perpendicular to the vector whose direction numbers are specified by $\{a, b, c\}$.* The analogous character of the equations of the plane and the line is easily seen by comparing (60) with (48). Furthermore, (60) may be written

$$ax + by + cz + d = 0, \qquad (61)$$

where $d = -(ax_0 + by_0 + cz_0)$, which is the counterpart of (49), and which clearly shows that the equation of a plane is linear in all three variables. Finally, it should be noted that the coefficients of the variables in both equations 49 and 61 are related to the perpendicular vectors **N**.

EXAMPLE 27. (a) What are the equations of the coordinate planes?

The xy-plane can be described as the plane perpendicular to **k** and passing through the origin. Therefore, its equation is found by simplifying $[(x - 0)\mathbf{i} + (y - 0)\mathbf{j} + (z - 0)\mathbf{k}] \cdot \mathbf{k} = 0$. The result is $z = 0$. Similarly, the reader can show that

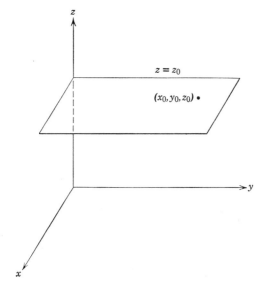

FIGURE 64

the equation for the yz-plane is $x = 0$, and the equation for xz-plane is $y = 0$.

(b) What are the equations of planes parallel to the coordinate planes?

We fix our attention on a plane parallel to the xy-plane and passing through (x_0, y_0, z_0), as shown in Figure 64. Then, following the same reasoning as in part (a), we arrive at $z = z_0$, which states that for all choices of x and y, the z-coordinate of a point on the plane is equal to z_0.

EXAMPLE 28. We shall discuss several questions relating to the plane whose equation is

$$2x + y - 2z - 2 = 0.$$

(a) To find a unit vector perpendicular to the given plane.

A vector perpendicular to the plane can immediately be written, by using the coefficients of the variables (see (60) or (61)), as

$$2\mathbf{i} + \mathbf{j} - 2\mathbf{k}.$$

Two unit vectors perpendicular to the plane are then

$$\pm \frac{2\mathbf{i} + \mathbf{j} - 2\mathbf{k}}{3}.$$

(b) What are the intercepts of the given locus? That is, what are the points at which the plane intersects the coordinate axes?

x-intercept. Since every point of the x-axis must have its y- and z-coordinates equal to zero, we solve for the x-coordinate of the intercept by placing $y = z = 0$ in the given equation of the plane. This gives $2x - 2 = 0$ or $x = 1$. Thus the x-intercept is $(1, 0, 0)$.

The reader can carry through the computation to verify that $(0, 2, 0)$ and $(0, 0, -1)$ are the other two intercepts.

(c) What are the *traces* of the plane whose equation is $2x + y - 2z - 2 = 0$, in the coordinate planes? We define the *trace* of a locus $\mathcal{L}$ in a plane Π to be the points of $\mathcal{L}$ that lie in Π, or simply the intersection of $\mathcal{L}$ and Π.

If we ask specifically for the trace in the xy-plane, we are asking for the locus satisfying the simultaneous equations

$$\begin{cases} 2x + y - 2z - 2 = 0 \\ z = 0 \quad (xy\text{-plane}). \end{cases}$$

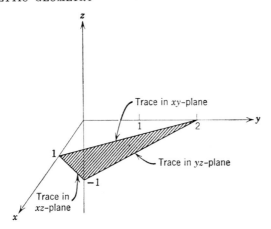

FIGURE 65

Thus, we would sketch the graph of $2x + y - 2 = 0$ in the xy-plane ($z = 0$) to see the trace in that plane. Again, the reader can verify that the other traces are obtained by graphing $x - z - 1 = 0$ and $y - 2z - 2 = 0$ in the xz-plane and yz-plane, respectively. Graphs of the traces in the coordinate plane are quite helpful in sketching a three-dimensional locus (see Figure 65).

23. DETERMINING A PLANE BY POINTS ON IT

How many points are actually necessary to determine a plane? Geometric intuition indicates that three points would be necessary and sufficient, but can this fact be shown algebraically?

If the four constants a, b, c, and d are known, the equation of the plane $ax + by + cz + d = 0$ is completely determined. This suggests that four, rather than three, conditions are necessary. However, our intuition did not lead us astray, for one of the four constants can be chosen to be unity. Not all of a, b, and c are zero, so we can divide through by one of them, say $a \neq 0$, and get

$$x + \frac{b}{a}y + \frac{c}{a}z + \frac{d}{a} = 0. \tag{62}$$

Making the substitution $\beta = b/a$, $\gamma = c/a$, and $\delta = d/a$, (62) becomes

$$x + \beta y + \gamma z + \delta = 0,$$

from which we see that there are essentially three constants to determine. In practice, it may turn out that $a = 0$, in which case the division just performed was illegal. If this be the case, then we could choose one of the other numbers as a divisor until we hit upon a legitimate division (see Example 30).

EXAMPLE 29. Find the plane through $(1, 2, 3)$, $(1, -1, 0)$, and $(2, -3, -4)$.

Assuming $d = 1$, we solve for a, b, and c in the equation

$$ax + by + cz + 1 = 0. \tag{63}$$

By imposing the condition that $(1, 2, 3)$ renders (63) true, we get

$$a + 2b + 3c + 1 = 0;$$

that $(1, -1, 0)$ renders (63) true yields

$$a - b + 1 = 0;$$

and that $(2, -3, 4)$ renders (63) true yields

$$2a - 3b - 4c + 1 = 0.$$

We can reduce this system of three equations in three unknowns to two equations in two unknowns most easily by using the second equation, which is already devoid of c, and then eliminating c from the first and third. To this end, we multiply the first by 4 and the third by 3, getting

$$4a + 8b + 12c + 4 = 0$$
$$6a - 9b - 12c + 3 = 0.$$

Addition yields

$$10a - b + 7 = 0,$$

which, together with $a - b + 1 = 0$, implies that

$$a = -\frac{2}{3} \quad \text{and} \quad b = \frac{1}{3}.$$

Substituting these values into the original equations gives $c = -\frac{1}{3}$. Therefore the desired line is $-\frac{2}{3}x + \frac{1}{3}y - \frac{1}{3}z + 1 = 0$, or more simply stated,

$$2x - y + z = 3.$$

EXAMPLE 30. Find the plane through $(0, 1, 2)$, $(1, -1, -2)$, and $(2, 2, 4)$.

Imposing the three points on equation 63 yields the system

$$b + 2c + 1 = 0$$

$$a - b - 2c + 1 = 0$$

$$2a + 2b + 4c + 1 = 0.$$

Adding the first two equations gives $a + 2 = 0$ or $a = -2$. However, adding twice the second equation to the third gives $4a + 3 = 0$ or $a = -\frac{3}{4}$, an inconsistency. So we must discard the assumption that $d \neq 0$. Instead, let us assume that $a \neq 0$; particularly that $a = 1$. Then we seek b, c, d in

$$x + by + cz + d = 0. \tag{64}$$

Imposing the three given points on relation (64), we get the system

$$b + 2c + d = 0 \tag{65}$$
$$1 - b - c + d = 0$$
$$2 + 2b + 4c + d = 0.$$

Adding the first two equations of (65) gives $1 + 2d = 0$ or $d = -\frac{1}{2}$; but adding twice the second to the third gives $4 + 3d = 0$ or $d = -\frac{4}{3}$, which is another inconsistency. So we discard the assumption that $a \neq 0$, upon which the form (64) was based. We now try $b \neq 0$, and use the form of the equation with $b = 1$

$$ax + y + cz + d = 0. \tag{66}$$

Once again we impose the given points, this time on (66), getting the system

$$1 + 2c + d = 0 \tag{67}$$
$$a - 1 - 2c + d = 0$$
$$2a + 2 + 4c + d = 0.$$

Adding the first two equations of (67) gives

$$a + 2d = 0, \qquad (68)$$

and adding twice the second to the third yields

$$4a + 3d = 0. \qquad (69)$$

Equations 68 and 69 now form a system of two equations in two unknowns, the solution of which is $a = d = 0$. Substituting back in (67) permits us to find that $c = -\frac{1}{2}$. Therefore we put these values in (66) and find the desired plane to be

$$y - \tfrac{1}{2}z = 0 \qquad \text{or} \qquad 2y - z = 0.$$

(Actually, the computation could have been simplified somewhat if we had set $d = 0$ after the appearance of the first inconsistency and then set $a = 0$ after the second inconsistency. However, this might have been jumping too far and too fast for an illustration.)

These cumbersome methods of finding the equation of a plane through three given points will be superseded by a far more simple and elegant vector approach in the next chapter.

24. DISTANCE FROM A POINT TO A PLANE

The problem of determining the distance from a given point $P_0 = (x_0, y_0, z_0)$ to a given plane

$$ax + by + cz + d = 0$$

is handled in precisely the same manner as was the earlier problem of finding the distance from a point to a line in the plane.

Call s the distance from P_0 to the given plane, and let $P = (x, y, z)$ be an arbitrary point of

$$ax + by + cz + d = 0$$

(see Figure 66). Then $s = |\mathrm{pr}_{\mathbf{N}}\overrightarrow{P_0P}|$, where $\mathbf{N}$ is a vector perpendicular to the plane. Let us—as before—

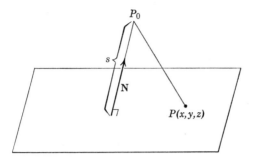

FIGURE 66

use a unit vector for $\mathbf{N}$. Then

$$\mathbf{N} = \frac{a\mathbf{i} + b\mathbf{j} + c\mathbf{k}}{\sqrt{a^2 + b^2 + c^2}}.$$

To determine the desired projection we resort to inner product

$$\left|\overrightarrow{P_0P} \cdot \mathbf{N}\right| = \left|\mathrm{pr}_{\mathbf{N}}\overrightarrow{P_0P}\right| = s.$$

Then

$$s = \left| \begin{aligned}[(x - x_0)\mathbf{i} + (y - y_0)\mathbf{j} \\ + (z - z_0)\mathbf{k}] \cdot \frac{a\mathbf{i} + b\mathbf{j} + c\mathbf{k}}{\sqrt{a^2 + b^2 + c^2}}\end{aligned} \right|$$

$$= \left| \frac{ax - ax_0 + by - by_0 + cz - cz_0}{\sqrt{a^2 + b^2 + c^2}} \right|.$$

But $ax + by + cz = -d$. Therefore,

$$s = \frac{\left|-ax_0 - by_0 - cz_0 - d\right|}{\sqrt{a^2 + br + c^2}} = \frac{\left|ax_0 + by_0 + cz_0 + d\right|}{\sqrt{a^2 + b^2 + c^2}}.$$

EXAMPLE 31. We find the distance from $P_0 = (1, -2, -3)$ to the plane whose equation is

$$x - 2y - 2z + 1 = 0.$$

Conforming to our policy of minimal memorization, we ignore the formula derived above and instead reason from first principles.

Since we seek the projection of $\overrightarrow{P_0P}$ on the perpendicular, where P is any point of the given plane, we shall find some particular P on $x - 2y - 2z + 1 = 0$, with which to work. One choice for P that would result in simple computation can be found by letting $y = z = 0$. Then, $x = -1$ and $P = (-1, 0, 0)$.
Therefore

$$s = |\text{pr}_\mathbf{N} \, \overrightarrow{P_0P}|$$

$$= \left| [(-1 - 1)\mathbf{i} + (0 - (-2))\mathbf{j} + (0 - (-3))\mathbf{k}] \right.$$

$$\left. \cdot \frac{\mathbf{i} - 2\mathbf{j} - 2\mathbf{k}}{\sqrt{1^2 + 2^2 + 2^2}} \right|$$

$$= \frac{|-2 - 4 - 6|}{3} = \frac{12}{3} = 4.$$

EXERCISES

1. Sketch the following planes, determining their intercepts and traces in the coordinate planes:
    (a) $x + 2y - z = 3$;
    (b) $x - z = 3$;
    (c) $2x - y + 2z + 9 = 0$;
    (d) $y = -3$.

2. Find the equation of the plane
    (a) through $(1, 1, 1)$, $(3, -2, 1)$, and $(2, -4, 3)$;
    (b) parallel to $-x + 2y - z = 5$ and through $(1, -1, 0)$;
    (c) perpendicular to $2\mathbf{i} - \mathbf{j} - \mathbf{k}$ and through the origin;
    (d) perpendicular to $2x + 3y - 6z = 12$, through the origin and $(2, 1, -4)$.
    (e) through $(-5, 0, 8)$ and perpendicular to a vector whose direction numbers are given by the set $\{4, -3, 12\}$.

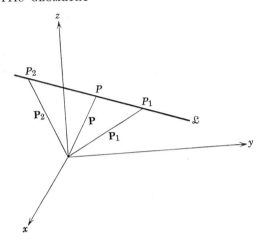

FIGURE 67

3. Find the distance from $(3, 0, -2)$ to
  (a) $3x + 4y - 12z = 52$,
  (b) $2x - y + 2z + 81 = 0$,
  (c) $4x - 3y = 100$.

25. THE STRAIGHT LINE IN THREE DIMENSIONS

Our discussion of the straight line in space shall follow the same pattern as the discussion of the line when our attention was confined to the plane.   We therefore begin by specifying a line $\mathcal{L}$ by two of its points $P_1 = (x_1, y_1, z_1)$ and seek an analytic representation of $\mathcal{L}$.

Let $P = (x, y, z)$ represent the general point of $\mathcal{L}$.

Applying Theorem 4 to the position vectors of the three collinear points (see Figure 67), we may write *the vector equation* of $\mathcal{L}$ as

$$\mathbf{P} = (1 - t)\mathbf{P}_1 + t\mathbf{P}_2. \tag{70}$$

In terms of the basis vectors, (70) becomes

$$x\mathbf{i} + y\mathbf{j} + z\mathbf{k} = (1 - t)x_1\mathbf{i} + (1 - t)y_1\mathbf{j}$$
$$+ (1 - t)z_1\mathbf{k} + tx_1\mathbf{i} + ty_2\mathbf{j} + tz_2\mathbf{k}$$
$$= [x_1 + t(x_2 - x_1)]\mathbf{i} + [y_1 + t(y_2 - y_1)]\mathbf{j}$$
$$+ [z_1 + t(z_2 - z_1)]\mathbf{k}.$$

Therefore

$$x = x_1 + t(x_2 - x_1)$$
$$y = y_1 + t(y_2 - y_1) \tag{71}$$
$$z = z_1 + t(z_2 - z_1).$$

is *the parametric representation of line $\mathcal{L}$ in analytic form.*

Elimination of the parameter t can be accomplished in a manner analogous to that in the discussion of the line in the plane. We solve for t in the parametric form, getting

$$\frac{x - x_1}{x_2 - x_1} = \frac{y - y_1}{y_2 - y_1} = \frac{z - z_1}{z_2 - z_1} = t.$$

Thus we may write the equation of $\mathcal{L}$ devoid of t as

$$\frac{x - x_1}{x_2 - x_1} = \frac{y - y_1}{y_2 - y_1} = \frac{z - z_1}{z_2 - z_1}, \tag{72}$$

which may be called the *two-point form of the line in three dimensions.*

The reader will observe that (72), which describes a locus in terms of coordinates and no auxiliary variable, is *not* a single equation. It actually consists of three equations, of which two are sufficient to deduce the third:

$$\frac{x - x_1}{x_2 - x_1} = \frac{y - y_1}{y_2 - y_1}, \quad \frac{x - x_1}{x_2 - x_1} = \frac{z - z_1}{z_2 - z_1},$$

$$\text{and} \quad \frac{y - y_1}{y_2 - y_1} = \frac{z - z_1}{z_2 - z_1}. \tag{73}$$

It may appear strange that more than one equation is necessary to describe a locus, but a moment's reflection makes it appear quite reasonable. For when we considered two simultaneous linear equations in plane analytic geometry, we stated that they defined a point, the point of intersection of two lines (if such existed). Each of the equations in (73) is linear and therefore defines a plane. Two of these considered simultaneously consist of the locus common to the two, namely, a line. That is, the intersection of two planes is a line. Each plane in (73) is parallel to one of the coordinate axes, but such special planes need not be the only ones used to define a line. In fact, any two simultaneous linear equations

$$\begin{cases} a_1 x + b_1 y + c_1 z + d_1 = 0 \\ a_2 x + b_2 y + c_2 z + d_2 = 0 \end{cases} \tag{74}$$

define a line unless the equations represent parallel planes. We shall have more to say later on such representations of lines.

The vector $\overrightarrow{P_1 P_2}$ that is parallel to (or along) line $\mathcal{L}$ is $\overrightarrow{P_1 P_2} = (x_2 - x_1)\mathbf{i} + (y_2 - y_1)\mathbf{j} + (z_2 - z_1)\mathbf{k}$ and therefore has a set of direction numbers $\{x_2 - x_1, y_2 - y_1, z_2 - z_1\}$. If the concept of *direction numbers* is applied to lines (see Figure 68), we see that the denominators in the two-point form (72) are precisely the direction numbers of the line. Given a set of direction numbers for $\mathcal{L}$, direction cosines for the line can be found by equations 58.

Let $\mathcal{L}_1$ be a line with direction numbers $\{l_1, m_1, n_1\}$ and $\mathcal{L}_2$ a line with direction numbers $\{l_2, m_2, n_2\}$. $\mathcal{L}_1$ is parallel to $\mathcal{L}_2$ if and only if vectors $\mathbf{V}_1 = l_1\mathbf{i} + m_1\mathbf{j} + n_1\mathbf{k}$ and $\mathbf{V}_2 = l_2\mathbf{i} + m_2\mathbf{j} + n_2\mathbf{k}$ are parallel. This latter condition is satisfied if and only if $\mathbf{V}_1$ is a (nonzero) multiple of $\mathbf{V}_2$, say

$$\mathbf{V}_1 = t\mathbf{V}_2,$$

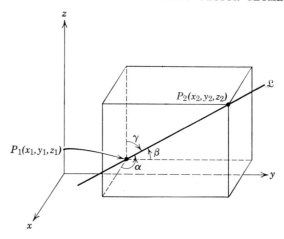

FIGURE 68

in which case $l_1 = tl_2$, $m_1 = tm_2$, and $n_1 = tn_2$ or

$$\frac{l_1}{l_2} = \frac{m_1}{m_2} = \frac{n_1}{n_2}. \tag{75}$$

Hence *a necessary and sufficient condition for lines* $\mathcal{L}_1$ *and* $\mathcal{L}_2$ *to be parallel is that their direction numbers be proportional.*

26. ANGLE BETWEEN TWO LINES

The angle between two lines is defined as the angle between two vectors, one parallel to each of the given lines. As a consequence of this definition, we may speak of the angle between two lines even if the lines do not intersect.

Considering the lines $\mathcal{L}_1$ and $\mathcal{L}_2$ as specified earlier, we shall derive a formula for the cosine of the angle θ between $\mathcal{L}_1$ and $\mathcal{L}_2$ in terms of the direction numbers of the lines.

The angle θ is the angle between $\mathbf{V}_1$ and $\mathbf{V}_2$, where $\mathbf{V}_1 = l_1\mathbf{i} + m_1\mathbf{j} + n_1\mathbf{k}$ and $\mathbf{V}_2 = l_2\mathbf{i} + m_2\mathbf{j} + n_2\mathbf{k}$. Using scalar products, we have

$$\cos \theta = \frac{\mathbf{V}_1 \cdot \mathbf{V}_2}{|\mathbf{V}_1|\,|\mathbf{V}_2|} = \frac{\mathbf{V}_1 \cdot \mathbf{V}_2}{\sqrt{\mathbf{V}_1 \cdot \mathbf{V}_1}\,\sqrt{\mathbf{V}_2 \cdot \mathbf{V}_2}},$$

or

$$\cos \theta = \frac{l_1 l_2 + m_1 m_2 + n_1 n_2}{\sqrt{l_1{}^2 + m_1{}^2 + n_1{}^2}\,\sqrt{l_2{}^2 + m_2{}^2 + n_2{}^2}}. \quad (76)$$

If the given direction numbers are direction cosines as well, (76) simplifies to become

$$\cos \theta = \cos \alpha_1 \cos \alpha_2 + \cos \beta_1 \cos \beta_2 + \cos \gamma_1 \cos \gamma_2. \quad (77)$$

As a corollary, we may conclude that the two lines are

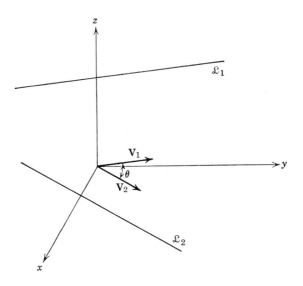

FIGURE 69

perpendicular if and only if

$$l_1 l_2 + m_1 m_2 + n_1 n_2 = 0. \tag{78}$$

EXAMPLE 32. Find the equation on the line $\mathcal{L}$ joining $P_1 = (2, -1, 3)$ to $P_2 = (1, 0, -5)$.

   (a) *Parametric Form.* From (71) we have

$$\mathcal{L}: \begin{cases} x = 2 + (1 - 2)t \\ y = -1 + (0 - (-1))t \\ z = 3 + (-5 - 3)t. \end{cases}$$

Simplifying yields

$$\mathcal{L}: \begin{cases} x = 2 - t \\ y = -1 + t \\ z = 3 - 8t. \end{cases}$$

We see that $\{-1, 1, 8\}$ is a set of direction numbers for $\mathcal{L}$.

A set of direction cosines is $\left\{ -\dfrac{1}{\sqrt{66}}, \dfrac{1}{\sqrt{66}}, \dfrac{8}{\sqrt{66}} \right\}$.

   (b) *Two-point form.* By means of (72) we have

$$\frac{x - 2}{-1} = \frac{y + 1}{1} = \frac{z - 3}{-8}.$$

EXAMPLE 33. Given line $\mathcal{L}': \dfrac{x - 1}{2} = \dfrac{y + 3}{-1} = z$, find (a)

a parametric representation of $\mathcal{L}'$; (b) the cosine of the angle θ between $\mathcal{L}'$ and line $\mathcal{L}$ of Example 32.

   (a) We set $\dfrac{x - 1}{2} = \dfrac{y + 3}{-1} = z = t$,

which can be restated as a parametric representation of $\mathcal{L}'$

$$x = 1 + 2t$$
$$y = -3 - t$$
$$z = t.$$

(*b*) A set of direction numbers for $\mathcal{L}'$ is $\{2, -1, 1\}$. We therefore apply (76), which gives

$$\cos \theta = \frac{-1(2) + 1(-1) + 8 \cdot 1}{\sqrt{(-1)^2 + 1^2 + 8^2} \sqrt{2^2 + (-1)^2 + 1^2}} = \frac{5}{6\sqrt{11}}.$$

EXAMPLE 34. Find the line $\mathcal{L}''$ parallel to $\mathcal{L}$ (of Example 32) and passing through $(1, 0, -2)$.

Since $\mathcal{L}''$ is parallel to $\mathcal{L}$, $\mathcal{L}''$ is of the form $\dfrac{x - x_1}{-1} = \dfrac{y - y_1}{1}$ $= \dfrac{z - z_1}{8}$, where (x_1, y_1, z_1) is a point of $\mathcal{L}''$. But $(1, 0, -2)$ is given as a point of $\mathcal{L}''$. Therefore the equations of the line are $\dfrac{x - 1}{-1} = y = \dfrac{z + 2}{8}.$

Thus far we have ignored the possibility of one of the direction numbers being zero, in which case the two-point form (72) could not apply because of the illegality of division by zero. Before proceeding with the algebraic problem involved, let us determine the geometric meaning of, say, the first direction number being zero. This would mean that $\cos \alpha = 0$, which implies $\alpha = \pi/2$. The line in question would therefore be perpendicular to the x-axis; or equivalently stated, the line would be parallel to (or actually in) the yz-plane. In summary, a line with a set of direction numbers $\{0, m, n\}$ is parallel to the yz-plane. Similarly, the reader can show that a line with a set of direction numbers $\{l, 0, n\}$ is parallel to the xz-plane; and a line with a set of direction numbers $\{l, m, 0\}$ is parallel to the xy-plane. If two of the direction numbers are zero, then the line is parallel to one of the axes.

EXAMPLE 35. Find equations of the line through $(1, 2, -1)$ and $(3, 2, -2)$.

A set of direction numbers is easily found to be $\{2, 0, -1\}$, so that the two-point form (72) cannot be used. However, a parametric form of the line can be written

$$x = 1 + 2t$$
$$y = 2$$
$$z = -1 - t.$$

Elimination of the parameter yields

$$\begin{cases} \dfrac{x - 1}{2} = \dfrac{z + 1}{-1} \\ y = 2, \end{cases}$$

which is a nonparametric form of the line and is as close as we may come to writing the two-point form. It is easy to see from both these representations that $y = 2$ no matter what the values of x and z are. That is, the line must be in the plane $y = 2$ and is, therefore, parallel to the xz-plane.

EXAMPLE 36. Find the equations for the line through $(1, -1, 2)$, with direction numbers given by the set $\{0, 4, 0\}$.

An equivalent set of direction numbers is $\{0, 1, 0\}$; indeed, $\{0, m, 0\}$ (when $m \neq 0$) is an equivalent set of direction numbers. We may thus write a parametric form as:

$$x = 1$$
$$y = -1 + t$$
$$z = 2.$$

Actually, the equation $y = -1 + t$ is quite superfluous, for the line is completely determined as the intersection of the planes $x = 1$ and $z = 2$. The y-coordinate may take on any value, which is what may happen in the foregoing parametric form of the line.

We now return to the representation of a line as the intersection of two planes (see equation 74). This idea has, of course, been employed throughout; for instance, in Example 35, (79) is the equation of a line in terms of two planes through it. Let us examine a more general case.

EXAMPLE 37. Given a line $\mathcal{L}$ whose algebraic representation is

$$2x + 3y - z = 1$$
$$x - y + z = 2,$$

we shall exhibit a method finding other forms for the equations of $\mathcal{L}$.

Eliminating z by adding the two equations gives

$$3x + 2y = 3.$$

Eliminating x from the given equations yields

$$5y - 3z = -3.$$

Solving for y in each of these allows us to write

$$\frac{3x - 3}{-2} = y = \frac{3z - 3}{5},$$

which may now be put in the form (72) by dividing numerator and denominator of the first and third members by 3:

$$\frac{x - 1}{-(2/3)} = y = \frac{z - 1}{5/3}. \tag{80}$$

Therefore a set of direction numbers is $\{-\frac{2}{3}, 1, \frac{5}{3}\}$.

By setting

$$\frac{x - 1}{-(2/3)} = y = \frac{z - 1}{5/3} = t,$$

we arrive at a parametric representation of the line

$$x = 1 - \frac{2}{3}t$$
$$y = t$$
$$z = 1 + \frac{5}{3}t.$$

EXERCISES

1. Find the equations, in two-point form, of the lines determined as follows:

(a) through $(-4, 1, -2)$ and parallel to z-axis;

(b) through $(-4, 1, -2)$ and $(5, 3, -1)$;

(c) through $(-4, 1, -2)$ and $(3, 1, 2)$;

(d) through $(3, 2, -5)$ and perpendicular to $3x - 2y - 6z = 1$;

(e) through $(3, 2, -5)$ and having $\cos \alpha = \frac{1}{9}$ and $\cos \beta = \frac{8}{9}$ (two possibilities);

(f) through $(-4, 1, -2)$ and having direction numbers 3, 4, 12;

(g) parallel to $5\mathbf{i} - 4\mathbf{j} + 6\mathbf{k}$ and through the origin.

2. Find parametric representations of the lines in Exercise 1.

3. Let AB, AC, and AD be three edges of a cube. Prove that plane through D and the line joining the midpoints of AB and AC is tangent to the sphere inscribed in the cube.

4. (a) Find a set of direction numbers for the line

$$\begin{cases} x - 3y + 7 = 0 \\ x - 2z - 4 = 0. \end{cases}$$

(b) Find a parametric representation for the line of part (a).

5. (a) Find equations of the form (72) that represent

$$3x - 2y - 6z = -9$$
$$x + 4y - 8z = -16.$$

(b) Find a parametric representation of the line of part (a).

6. Prove that the following are vertices of a right triangle:
(a) $(0, 7, 6)$, $(-2, 1, 3)$, $(6, 4, 8)$;
(b) $(0, -2, 4)$, $(-3, -4, -2)$, $(2, 4, 1)$.

7. Three vertices of a parallelogram in order are $(4, 3, 5)$, $(0, 6, 0)$, and $(-8, 1, 4)$. Find the fourth vertex.

8. Find the direction cosines of a line perpendicular, simultaneously, to

$$\frac{x - 1}{2} = \frac{y - 1}{3} = \frac{z - 1}{6} \quad \text{and} \quad \frac{x}{3} = \frac{y}{4} = \frac{z}{12}.$$

9. Find the cosine of the angles made by the two lines of Exercise 8.

27. INTERSECTION OF A LINE WITH A PLANE

Since a line may be represented by the equations of two planes through it, the point of intersection (if there is one) of the line with a plane may be found by solving the three linear equations simultaneously. However, we illustrate another method for solving this problem by utilizing the parametric representation of the line.

EXAMPLE 38.   Find the point of intersection of the line

$$\mathscr{L}: \begin{cases} 2x + 3y - z = 1 \\ x - y + z = 2 \end{cases}$$

and the plane

$$\Pi: x + 2y - 2z = -3.$$

Solving these three linear equations simultaneously yields $(\frac{1}{3}, 1, \frac{8}{3})$ as the point of intersection. However, for the alternative approach, we use the parametric form of $\mathscr{L}$:

$$x = 1 - \tfrac{2}{3}t$$

$$y = t$$

$$z = 1 + \tfrac{5}{3}t,$$

which was found in Example 37.

Substituting these equations in the equation of plane Π gives $(1 - \frac{2}{3}t) + 2t - 2(1 + \frac{5}{3}t) = -3$, the solution of which will give the value of the parameter t, which yields the point of $\mathscr{L}$ that is also on Π (see Figure 70). This value is $t = 1$. Thus, the point we seek is given by $x = \frac{1}{3}$, $y = 1$, $z = \frac{8}{3}$.

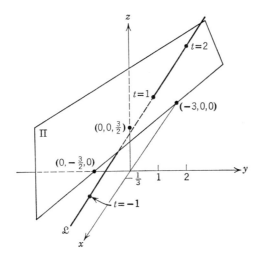

FIGURE 70

28. ANGLE BETWEEN A LINE AND A PLANE

How can we extend our understanding of the angle of intersection of a pair of lines to define the concept of the *angle between a line and a plane?* If $\mathcal{L}$ is the line and Π the plane, there are an infinity of lines $\mathcal{L}_\pi$ in the plane Π that might conceivably be used to find an angle between $\mathcal{L}$ and Π (see Figure 71). Since such an infinity of choices for the angle between a line and a plane is undesirable, the one usually selected as *the* angle of intersection between $\mathcal{L}$ and Π is the minimum angle β of the infinity formed by $\mathcal{L}$ and the lines $\mathcal{L}_\pi$. However, such a definition renders the problem of finding β extremely difficult—indeed, impossible at this point. We therefore turn to the more convenient definition: The *angle β between line $\mathcal{L}$ and plane* Π is defined to be the complement of the angle between $\mathcal{L}$ and a line $\mathfrak{N}$ perpendicular to Π.

EXAMPLE 39. Find the angle of intersection between the line $\mathcal{L}$ and the plane Π of Example 38.

A vector parallel to $\mathcal{L}$ is $\mathbf{L} = -\frac{2}{3}\mathbf{i} + \mathbf{j} + \frac{5}{3}\mathbf{k}$. A vector perpendicular to plane Π is $\mathbf{N} = \mathbf{i} + 2\mathbf{j} - 2\mathbf{k}$. Thus the comple-

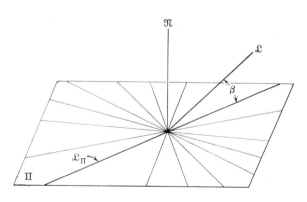

FIGURE 71

ment of β may be found by dot products

$$\cos\left(\frac{\pi}{2} - \beta\right) = \frac{|-2/3 + 2 - 10/3|}{\sqrt{39/9}\,\sqrt{9}} = \frac{2}{\sqrt{39}},$$

which is equivalent to $\sin \beta = 2/\sqrt{39}$.

EXERCISES

1. In the computation of Example 39, we were careful to take the absolute value of the numerator in the determination of $\cos\left(\frac{\pi}{2} - \beta\right)$. Why?

This indicates that our definition of β has a slight shortcoming, which the reader should eliminate by a small modification of the definition.

2. Find a general formula for the $\sin \beta$, where β is the angle formed by a line meeting a plane.

3. Using two different methods, find the coordinates of the point of intersection of line, with a representation

$$\frac{x - 3}{2} = \frac{y + 2}{-1} = \frac{z - 3}{3}$$

and the plane whose equation is $3x + 2y - z = 5$.

4. Find the angle between the line and plane given in Exercise 3 above.

5. Find the point of intersection and the angle of intersection of the line and plane whose equations are

$$\frac{x + 3}{2} = \frac{y + 3}{3} = \frac{z + 3}{6}$$

and $\qquad 10x + 2y - 11z = 3.$

6. (a) Give a suitable definition for the angle between two planes.

(b) Find a general formula for the angle between two planes, whose equations are

$$a_1x + b_1y + c_1z + d_1 = 0$$

and
$$a_2x + b_2y + c_2z + d_2 = 0.$$

(*Hint.* Use two vectors, each perpendicular to one of the given planes.)

(c) Find the angle made by the intersection of the planes whose equations are $2x + 2y + z = 1$ and $2x + 10y - 11z = 3$.

(d) Find the angle between the two planes whose equations are $x - 4y + 8z = 2$ and $2x + y - 2z = 18$.

7. Show that the line given by

$$\begin{cases} x - 3y + 7 = 0 \\ x - 2z = 4, \end{cases}$$

(a) is parallel to the plane whose equation is $3x - 6y - 2z = 0$,

(b) lies in the plane whose equation is $12x + 4y + 6z = 1$.

8. Apply fundamental vector techniques to the following problems.

(a) Find the angle between the diagonal of a cube and one of its edges.

(b) Find the angle between the diagonal of a cube and a diagonal of one of its faces.

(c) Find the angle between the diagonal of a cube and one of its faces.

5

cross
products

29. CROSS PRODUCTS

As we have seen, the inner product of two vectors yields a scalar quantity, hence the synonym scalar product. In the present section we introduce another kind of multiplication of vectors, which leads to (1) a vector quantity and (2) a relation involving the sine of the angle between two vectors (as opposed to the appearance of the cosine in dot products). Since, by now, the reader has gained some security in dealing with vectors, we take the liberty of a longer excursion through the algebra of cross products before illustrating the theory.

Definition of cross product. Let $\mathbf{A}$ and $\mathbf{B}$ be any two vectors, and call θ the smaller angle between them. Then the *cross product* of $\mathbf{A}$ and $\mathbf{B}$, denoted $\mathbf{A} \times \mathbf{B}$, is a vector

$$|\mathbf{A}|\,|\mathbf{B}|\sin\theta\,\mathbf{U}, \tag{81}$$

where $\mathbf{U}$ is a unit vector perpendicular to the plane of

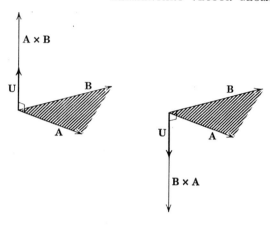

FIGURE 72

A and **B**, and pointed in such direction as to make {**A**, **B**, **U**} a right-handed triple. That is, if the observer who walks from the terminus of **A** to the terminus of **B** through the angle θ (when the two vectors both emanate from a single point O) always has O to his left, then he is always standing upright parallel to **U**, with his "upward direction" being precisely the direction of **U**. Thus, {**A**, **B**, **A** ✕ **B**} form a right-handed triple if none of the three vectors are the zero vector, for **A** ✕ **B** (if non-null) points in the same direction as **U**. This assertion follows from the fact that the coefficient of **U** in (81) cannot be negative because $0 \leq \sin \theta \leq 1$ when $0 \leq \theta \leq \pi$, and lengths of vectors are non-negative scalars.

Because the cross product results in a vector quantity, it is often termed the *vector product*. We shall continue our earlier policy of utilizing both names so that the reader will become familiar with all the standard—and equally popular—terminologies.

An immediate corollary of the definition is that the vector product defines a noncommutative multiplication.

In fact, we have the

Theorem 8. $A \times B = -B \times A$.

This result follows quite simply from the observation that $B \times A$ has the same magnitude as $A \times B$ but points in the opposite direction (see Figure 72).

Query: Suppose the word "smaller" were left out of the definition of vector product. Would the resulting definition be equivalent to the original one?

Attempting to gain further physical or geometric insight into the notion of cross product, we observe that

$$A \text{ is parallel to } B \text{ implies } A \times B = O; \qquad (82)$$

for if A and B are parallel, then $\theta = 0$ and $\sin \theta = 0$. (Is the converse of (82) true?) A geometric interpretation of the magnitude of the cross product is given by

Theorem 9. *The area of the parallelogram generated by vectors A and B is equal to $|A \times B|$.*

Proof. (See Figure 73.) The area of the parallelogram generated by A and B is equal to

$$|A|h = |A| \, |B| \sin \theta = |A \times B|.$$

30. TRIPLE SCALAR PRODUCT

The product $A \cdot B \times C$ is called the *triple scalar product* of A, B, and C.

N.B. (1) Although parentheses might appear necessary—at least to assist the beginner—to indicate which operation (the "cross" or the "dot") is performed first, it should be noted that such parentheses would be com-

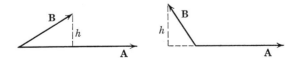

FIGURE 73

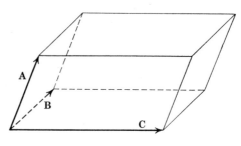

FIGURE 74

pletely superfluous, for there is only one possible logical order for the two operations. "Cross" must precede "dot"; otherwise we would have a scalar crossed with a vector, which has no meaning for us.

(2) The product $\mathbf{A} \times \mathbf{B} \cdot \mathbf{C}$ also yields a scalar quantity and thus is also called the triple scalar product of $\mathbf{A}, \mathbf{B},$ and $\mathbf{C}$ (in that order). Calling both quantities, $\mathbf{A} \cdot \mathbf{B} \times \mathbf{C}$ and $\mathbf{A} \times \mathbf{B} \cdot \mathbf{C}$, *the* triple scalar product would be reasonable and warranted only if they were always equal—and so they are, as we shall soon see.

Theorem 10. *The magnitude of* $\mathbf{A} \cdot \mathbf{B} \times \mathbf{C}$ *represents the volume V of the parallelepiped generated by the vectors* $\mathbf{A}, \mathbf{B},$ *and* $\mathbf{C}$.

Proof. (See Figure 74.)

$$|\mathbf{B} \times \mathbf{C}| = \text{area of base (Theorem 9)}$$
and $|\mathbf{A}| \cos \alpha = \pm \text{ altitude of parallelepiped.}$

Therefore $\pm V = |\mathbf{A}| \, |\mathbf{B} \times \mathbf{C}| \cos \alpha$, which states that $V = |\mathbf{A} \cdot \mathbf{B} \times \mathbf{C}|$.

The reader should investigate the question of sign by answering the following question: What kind of orientation of $\mathbf{A}, \mathbf{B},$ and $\mathbf{C}$ leads to a positive triple scalar product? What kind to a negative triple scalar product?

In which case does the triple scalar product equal V and in which case does it equal $-V$?

Corollary. $\mathbf{A} \cdot \mathbf{B} \times \mathbf{C} = \mathbf{A} \times \mathbf{B} \cdot \mathbf{C}$.

Proof. Since both triple scalar products represent the same volume, and since the sign depends only on the orientation of the triple $\{\mathbf{A}, \mathbf{B}, \mathbf{C}\}$, the two products must be equal.

Our final result on the algebra of vector products is embodied in the following theorem.

Theorem 11. *The vector product is distributive with respect to addition. That is,*

$$\text{(i) } \mathbf{A} \times (\mathbf{B} + \mathbf{C}) = \mathbf{A} \times \mathbf{B} + \mathbf{A} \times \mathbf{C}, \text{ and}$$
$$\text{(ii) } (\mathbf{A} + \mathbf{B}) \times \mathbf{C} = \mathbf{A} \times \mathbf{C} + \mathbf{B} \times \mathbf{C}.$$

Proof of (i). Let

$$\mathbf{D} = \mathbf{A} \times (\mathbf{B} + \mathbf{C}) - \mathbf{A} \times \mathbf{B} - \mathbf{A} \times \mathbf{C}.$$

Our proof will be completed if we can show that $\mathbf{D}$ is necessarily the zero vector.

We take the scalar product of $\mathbf{D}$ with an *arbitrary* vector $\mathbf{V}$.

$$\mathbf{V} \cdot \mathbf{D} = \mathbf{V} \cdot [\mathbf{A} \times (\mathbf{B} + \mathbf{C}) - \mathbf{A} \times \mathbf{B} - \mathbf{A} \times \mathbf{C}]$$

$$= \mathbf{V} \cdot \mathbf{A} \times (\mathbf{B} + \mathbf{C}) - \mathbf{V} \cdot \mathbf{A} \times \mathbf{B} - \mathbf{V} \cdot \mathbf{A} \times \mathbf{C}$$
$$\text{(Theorem 7)}$$

$$= \mathbf{V} \times \mathbf{A} \cdot (\mathbf{B} + \mathbf{C}) - \mathbf{V} \times \mathbf{A} \cdot \mathbf{B} - \mathbf{V} \times \mathbf{A} \cdot \mathbf{C}$$
$$\text{(Corollary to Theorem 10).}$$

Now, using the distributivity of dot products on the first term of the right member, we get

$$\mathbf{V} \cdot \mathbf{D} = \mathbf{V} \times \mathbf{A} \cdot \mathbf{B} + \mathbf{V} \times \mathbf{A} \cdot \mathbf{C} - \mathbf{V} \times \mathbf{A} \cdot \mathbf{B}$$
$$- \mathbf{V} \times \mathbf{A} \cdot \mathbf{C}.$$

Hence

$$\mathbf{V} \cdot \mathbf{D} = 0. \tag{83}$$

Recalling that **V** is arbitrary, we see then that (83) states that the vector **D** is perpendicular to any vector. Consequently, **D** = **O** and we have

$$\mathbf{A} \times (\mathbf{B} + \mathbf{C}) = \mathbf{A} \times \mathbf{B} + \mathbf{A} \times \mathbf{C}.$$

Part (ii) is left as an exercise, for it follows readily from (i) and Theorem 8.

We are now in possession of sufficient tools to develop a formula for the cross product of two vectors that are represented in terms of our $\{\mathbf{i}, \mathbf{j}, \mathbf{k}\}$-basis. First, we note that

$$\mathbf{i} \times \mathbf{i} = \mathbf{j} \times \mathbf{j} = \mathbf{k} \times \mathbf{k} = \mathbf{O}. \qquad (84)$$

Applying the definition (81), we further see that

$$\mathbf{i} \times \mathbf{j} = \mathbf{k}, \quad \mathbf{j} \times \mathbf{k} = \mathbf{i}, \quad \text{and } \mathbf{k} \times \mathbf{i} = \mathbf{j}, \qquad (85)$$

and imposing Theorem 8 on the relations of (85) yields

$$\mathbf{j} \times \mathbf{i} = -\mathbf{k}, \quad \mathbf{k} \times \mathbf{j} = -\mathbf{i}, \quad \text{and } \mathbf{i} \times \mathbf{k} = -\mathbf{j}. \qquad (86)$$

Now let

$$\mathbf{A} = a_1\mathbf{i} + a_2\mathbf{j} + a_3\mathbf{k} \qquad \text{and} \qquad \mathbf{B} = b_1\mathbf{i} + b_2\mathbf{j} + b_3\mathbf{k}.$$

Then

$$\begin{aligned}
\mathbf{A} \times \mathbf{B} &= (a_1\mathbf{i} + a_2\mathbf{j} + a_3\mathbf{k}) \times (b_1\mathbf{i} + b_2\mathbf{j} + b_3\mathbf{k}) \\
&= (a_1\mathbf{i} + a_2\mathbf{j} + a_3\mathbf{k}) \times b_1\mathbf{i} \\
&\quad + (a_1\mathbf{i} + a_2\mathbf{j} + a_3\mathbf{k}) \times b_2\mathbf{j} \\
&\quad\quad + (a_1\mathbf{i} + a_2\mathbf{j} + a_3\mathbf{k}) \times b_3\mathbf{k} \\
&= a_1\mathbf{i} \times b_1\mathbf{i} + a_2\mathbf{j} \times b_1\mathbf{i} + a_3\mathbf{k} \times b_1\mathbf{i} \\
&\quad + a_1\mathbf{i} \times b_2\mathbf{j} + a_2\mathbf{j} \times b_2\mathbf{j} + a_3\mathbf{k} \times b_2\mathbf{j} \\
&\quad\quad + a_1\mathbf{i} \times b_3\mathbf{k} + a_2\mathbf{j} \times b_3\mathbf{k} + a_3\mathbf{k} \times b_3\mathbf{k}.
\end{aligned}$$

By using (84), (85), and (86), we simplify this expansion to obtain

$$\mathbf{A} \times \mathbf{B} = (a_2b_3 - a_3b_2)\mathbf{i} + (a_3b_1 - a_1b_3)\mathbf{j} + (a_1b_2 - a_2b_1)\mathbf{k}. \qquad (87)$$

The reader who is familiar with determinants will be pleased to see how convenient it is to express the formula for $\mathbf{A} \times \mathbf{B}$ in the language of determinants.[1] Equation (87) states

$$\mathbf{A} \times \mathbf{B} = \mathbf{i} \begin{vmatrix} a_2 & a_3 \\ b_2 & b_3 \end{vmatrix} - \mathbf{j} \begin{vmatrix} a_1 & a_3 \\ b_1 & b_3 \end{vmatrix} + \mathbf{k} \begin{vmatrix} a_1 & a_2 \\ b_1 & b_2 \end{vmatrix}$$

or, more simply

$$\mathbf{A} \times \mathbf{B} = \begin{vmatrix} \mathbf{i} & \mathbf{j} & \mathbf{k} \\ a_1 & a_2 & a_3 \\ b_1 & b_2 & b_3 \end{vmatrix}. \tag{88}$$

EXAMPLE 40. Our first illustration of the use of cross products will be to apply this concept to the problem of Example 28, namely, that of finding a vector perpendicular to the plane whose equation is $2x + y - 2z - 2 = 0$.

Since the cross product of two vectors is a vector perpendicular to the plane of the given two, we need only determine two vectors in the plane $2x + y - 2z - 2 = 0$ and take their cross product. We therefore select three points, arbitrarily in the given plane: $A = (0, 0, -1)$, $B = (0, 2, 0)$, $C = (1, 0, 0)$. Then $\overrightarrow{AB} = 2\mathbf{j} + \mathbf{k}$ and $\overrightarrow{AC} = \mathbf{i} + \mathbf{k}$.
Hence

$$\overrightarrow{AB} \times \overrightarrow{AC} = \begin{vmatrix} \mathbf{i} & \mathbf{j} & \mathbf{k} \\ 0 & 2 & 1 \\ 1 & 0 & 1 \end{vmatrix} = 2\mathbf{i} + \mathbf{j} - 2\mathbf{k}$$

is a vector perpendicular to the plane of A, B, and C. (It is reassuring to note that this answer agrees with the one found in our first solution to this problem).

Although the area of a triangle is a simple theoretical problem, it is quite often a cumbersome task to compute an area by the usual formulas when given the coordinates of the vertices. We exhibit the power of vector products in attacking such a problem as

[1] For the reader who is unfamiliar with determinants, we have a brief word of assistance in the appendix.

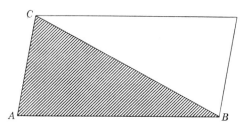

FIGURE 75

EXAMPLE 41. Let the vertices of a triangle be given by

$$A = (1, -5, 2), \quad B = (-2, 3, -1), \quad \text{and } C = (5, 0, 2).$$

Then $\overrightarrow{AB} = 3\mathbf{i} + 8\mathbf{j} - 3\mathbf{k}$ and $\overrightarrow{AC} = 4\mathbf{i} + 5\mathbf{j}$.

$$\overrightarrow{AB} \times \overrightarrow{AC} = \begin{vmatrix} \mathbf{i} & \mathbf{j} & \mathbf{k} \\ -3 & 8 & -3 \\ 4 & 5 & 0 \end{vmatrix} = 15\mathbf{i} - 12\mathbf{j} + 17\mathbf{k}.$$

Since $|\overrightarrow{AB} \times \overrightarrow{AC}|$ equals the area of the parallelogram (see Figure 75), three of whose vertices are A, B, and C, the area K of the shaded triangle we desire is precisely $\frac{1}{2}|\overrightarrow{AB} \times \overrightarrow{AC}|$. Therefore

$$\text{K} = \tfrac{1}{2}|15\mathbf{i} - 12\mathbf{j} + 17\mathbf{k}| = \tfrac{1}{2}\sqrt{658}.$$

In our earlier work we solved, by analytic methods, the problem of determining the equation of a plane through three given points. The vector approach to this problem is demonstrated in the next example.

EXAMPLE 42. Find the plane through $A = (1, 2, 3)$, $B = (1, -1, 0)$, and $C = (2, -3, -4)$. (The analytic solution to this problem was given in Example 29.) The vector $\overrightarrow{AB} \times \overrightarrow{AC}$ is perpendicular to the desired plane and is therefore perpendicular to every vector in the desired plane (see

Figure 76). Hence $P = (x, y, z)$ is a general point in the plane if and only if $\overrightarrow{BP} \cdot \overrightarrow{AB} \times \overrightarrow{AC} = 0$.

Writing this condition explicitly gives
$$[(x - 1)\mathbf{i} + (y + 1)\mathbf{j} + z\mathbf{k}] \cdot (-3\mathbf{j} - 3\mathbf{k}) \times (\mathbf{i} - 5\mathbf{j} - 7\mathbf{k}) = 0.$$
In terms of determinants, this relation becomes

$$\begin{vmatrix} x - 1 & y + 1 & z \\ 0 & -3 & -3 \\ 1 & -5 & -7 \end{vmatrix} = 0;$$

or, expanding by means of the formulas for cross product and dot product, we get $-2x + y - z + 3 = 0$ as the equation of the plane determined by A, B, and C.

31. DISTANCE FROM A POINT TO A PLANE

The distance from a point to a plane was found by projecting on a unit perpendicular to the plane. But now this procedure may be facilitated, for by means of cross products, the unit perpendicular to a plane may be found directly from three points of the plane without any need for determining the equation of the plane.

EXAMPLE 43. Let a plane be determined by the points $A = (-3, 0, 1)$, $B = (-1, 1, -1)$, and $C = (2, 1, \frac{1}{2})$; and let $P = (1, -2, -3)$. We shall determine the distance d from P_0 to the plane of A, B, and C. (The reader is referred to Example 31, which is the present problem in disguise).

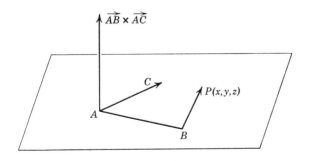

FIGURE 76

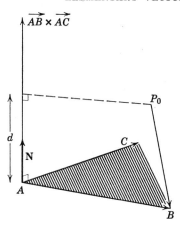

FIGURE 77

A vector perpendicular to the given plane may be found by taking the cross product $\overrightarrow{AB} \times \overrightarrow{AC}$ (see Figure 77, which symbolizes the geometry)

$$\overrightarrow{AB} \times \overrightarrow{AC} = \begin{vmatrix} \mathbf{i} & \mathbf{j} & \mathbf{k} \\ 2 & 1 & 0 \\ 5 & 1 & \frac{3}{2} \end{vmatrix} = \tfrac{3}{2}\mathbf{i} - 3\mathbf{j} - 3\mathbf{k} = 3(\tfrac{1}{2}\mathbf{i} - \mathbf{j} - \mathbf{k}).$$

Then a unit perpendicular is

$$\mathbf{N} = \frac{\overrightarrow{AB} \times \overrightarrow{AC}}{|AB \times AC|} = \frac{\tfrac{1}{2}\mathbf{i} - \mathbf{j} - \mathbf{k}}{\sqrt{\tfrac{1}{4} + 1 + 1}} = \frac{1}{3}(\mathbf{i} - 2\mathbf{j} - 2\mathbf{k})$$

(Compare with Example 31.)

$$\begin{aligned} d &= |\mathrm{pr}_{\mathbf{N}}\,\overrightarrow{P_0B}| = |\overrightarrow{P_0B} \cdot \mathbf{N}| \\ &= |(-2\mathbf{i} + 3\mathbf{j} + 2\mathbf{k}) \cdot \tfrac{1}{3}(\mathbf{i} - 2\mathbf{j} - 2\mathbf{k})| = \tfrac{1}{3}(2 + 6 + 4) \\ &= 4. \end{aligned}$$

32. DISTANCE BETWEEN TWO LINES

We now direct attention to one of the nastiest problems of elementary analytic geometry, namely, the problem of finding the distance between two nonintersecting lines of space. We refer to this as a nasty problem because, if pure analytic geometry is the means of analysis, the beginning student is usually plagued by the problem of visualization that is required to "see" the derivation of the formula, and then he is plagued by another complicated formula to memorize. Once again, the vector approach assists with both difficulties.

If two lines $\mathcal{L}_1$ and $\mathcal{L}_2$ are given, the minimum distance d between them is the distance between $\mathcal{L}_1$ and $\mathcal{L}_2$ along the mutual perpendicular (QR in Figure 78). Thus, if we call A and B points of $\mathcal{L}_1$ and $\mathcal{L}_2$, respectively,

$$d = \left| \mathrm{pr}_{\overrightarrow{QR}} \overrightarrow{AB} \right|.$$

(Readers who have difficulty understanding this point are encouraged to check back on the definition of projection.) The procedure for computing d is given in the following example.

EXAMPLE 44. Let $\mathcal{L}_1 = AC$, where $A = (2, -1, 3)$ and $C = (1, 0, -5)$; and let $\mathcal{L}_2 = BD$, where $B = (1, 3, 0)$ and $D = (3, -4, 1)$. We shall determine the distance between $\mathcal{L}_1$ and $\mathcal{L}_2$.

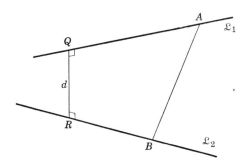

FIGURE 78

A vector that is simultaneously perpendicular to $\mathcal{L}_1$ and $\mathcal{L}_2$ is

$$\mathbf{N} = \overrightarrow{AC} \times \overrightarrow{BD} = \begin{vmatrix} \mathbf{i} & \mathbf{j} & \mathbf{k} \\ -1 & 1 & -8 \\ 2 & -7 & 1 \end{vmatrix} = 55\mathbf{i} - 15\mathbf{j} + 5\mathbf{k}.$$

Then

$$\begin{aligned} d = \left| \mathrm{pr}_{\mathbf{N}} \overrightarrow{AB} \right| &= \left| AB \cdot \frac{\mathbf{N}}{|\mathbf{N}|} \right| \\ &= \frac{|(-\mathbf{i} + 4\mathbf{j} - 3\mathbf{k}) \cdot 5(11\mathbf{i} - 3\mathbf{j} + \mathbf{k})|}{5 \sqrt{121 + 9 + 1}} \\ &= \frac{|-11 - 12 - 3|}{\sqrt{131}} = \frac{26}{\sqrt{131}}. \end{aligned}$$

EXERCISES

1. Evaluate the following
   (a) $\mathbf{i} \times (\mathbf{j} + \mathbf{k})$,
   (b) $(\mathbf{i} + \mathbf{j}) \times \mathbf{k}$,
   (c) $(\mathbf{i} + \mathbf{j} + \mathbf{k}) \times (\mathbf{i} + \mathbf{j} + \mathbf{k})$,
   (d) $(2\mathbf{i} - 3\mathbf{j} + \mathbf{k}) \times (2\mathbf{j} - \mathbf{k})$,
   (e) $(-\mathbf{i} + 2\mathbf{j} + 4\mathbf{k}) \times (\mathbf{i} + 2\mathbf{j} + 4\mathbf{k})$.

2. Using the fact that a parallelepiped can be sliced into six tetrahedra of equal volume, determine a formula for the volume of a tetrahedron, the four vertices of which are $A = (a_1, a_2 \ a_3)$, $B = (b_1, b_2, b_3)$, $C = (c_1, c_2, c_3)$, and $D = (d_1, d_2, d_3)$.

3. Find the volume of a regular pyramid whose base is a square of side a and whose height is h. (*A pyramid is called regular when its base is a regular polygon and when the altitude from the apex meets the base in its center.*)

4. Prove that the answer to Exercise 3 is unchanged if the second condition of "regular" is omitted. That is, a change in the position of the apex does not alter the volume of the pyramid as long as the apex remains at a fixed height h above the base.

5. Determine the equation of the line $\mathcal{L}$ through $P_0 = (x_0, y_0, z_0)$ and parallel to $\mathbf{V} = l\mathbf{i} + m\mathbf{j} + n\mathbf{k}$ by observing that $\overrightarrow{P_0P} \times \mathbf{V} = \mathbf{O}$, where $P = (x, y, z)$ is any point of $\mathcal{L}$.

6. (a) If $P = (x, y, z)$ is an arbitrary point of plane ABC, justify the equation $\overrightarrow{AP} \cdot \overrightarrow{AB} \times \overrightarrow{AC} = 0$ as being a vector equation of the plane. (See Example 42.)

(b) Using the method of part (a), derive the equation of the plane determined by $A = (1, 0, 0)$, $B = (0, 1, 0)$, and $C = (0, 0, 1)$.

7. Using the methods of this chapter, determine a vector formula for the distance from the origin to plane ABC.

8. Let **U** and **V** be parallel to plane Π_1, while **W** and **Y** are parallel to plane Π_2. Under the further assumption that $\Pi_1 \perp \Pi_2$, prove $(\mathbf{U} \times \mathbf{V}) \cdot (\mathbf{W} \times \mathbf{Y}) = 0$.

9. Find the distance between

(a) $x = 1 - 2t, \quad y = t, \quad z = -t$
   and $x = t, \quad y = 1 - 2t, \quad z = -t.$

(b) $\dfrac{x - 1}{2} = \dfrac{y}{2} = z + 1$

   and $\dfrac{x}{2} = \dfrac{y + 2}{-1} = z.$

(c) line AB and line CD, where $A = (0, 1, 2)$, $B = (1, -1, 4)$, $C = (0, 2, 0)$, and $D = (-1, 2, 2)$.

10. If **C** is perpendicular to the plane of **A** and **B**, prove that $(\mathbf{A} \times \mathbf{B}) \cdot (\mathbf{C} \times \mathbf{D}) = 0$.

11. Find a set of direction numbers for the line of intersection of the planes whose equations are $a_1x + b_1y + c_1z + d_1 = 0$ and $a_2x + b_2y + c_2z + d_2 = 0$, by a direct application of cross products.

33. TRIPLE CROSS PRODUCTS

For the application of vector algebra to more complex problems of geometry and, particularly, to the development of trigonometry—as the reader will see in the next chapter—we shall find it useful to expand cross products of three and more vectors.

We begin by obtaining an expansion for the triple vector product $A \times (B \times C)$. Unfortunately, there is no simple and well-motivated development for such a formula. A summary of the efforts of several mathematicians who have contributed to various simplifications of the problem appears in a short paper, "On the Vector Triple Product," by Murrey S. Klamkin (*American Mathematical Monthly*, December 1954). We adopt an approach, the virtue of which is simplicity.

If we are given the three vectors A, B, and C, we consider the three emanating from a point O, which is taken to be the origin of a rectangular coordinate system. We impose the coordinate system in the following way (see Figure 79):

(i) the x-axis is taken along B;

(ii) the y-axis is taken in the plane of B and C;

(iii) the z-axis is taken so that the xyz-coordinate system, with $\{i, j, k\}$ as a basis, is right-handed.

It follows from (i) that $B = b_1 i$, and from (ii) that $C = c_1 i + c_2 j$. Since A is free from any stipulation, it

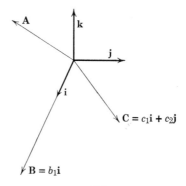

FIGURE 79

must be written $\mathbf{A} = a_1\mathbf{i} + a_2\mathbf{j} + a_3\mathbf{k}$.   Then

$$\mathbf{B} \times \mathbf{C} = \begin{vmatrix} \mathbf{i} & \mathbf{j} & \mathbf{k} \\ b_1 & 0 & 0 \\ c_1 & c_2 & 0 \end{vmatrix} = b_1 c_2 \mathbf{k},$$

and

$$\mathbf{A} \times (\mathbf{B} \times \mathbf{C}) = \begin{vmatrix} \mathbf{i} & \mathbf{j} & \mathbf{k} \\ a_1 & a_2 & a_3 \\ 0 & 0 & b_1 c_2 \end{vmatrix} = a_2 b_1 c_2 \mathbf{i} - a_1 b_1 c_2 \mathbf{j}. \quad (89)$$

We observe that $\mathbf{A} \times (\mathbf{B} \times \mathbf{C})$ must be perpendicular to $\mathbf{B} \times \mathbf{C}$, that is, $\mathbf{A} \times (\mathbf{B} \times \mathbf{C})$ is perpendicular to the coordinate vector $\mathbf{k}$.   Thus the triple cross product, $\mathbf{A} \times (\mathbf{B} \times \mathbf{C})$, must be in the plane of $\mathbf{B}$ and $\mathbf{C}$.   Hence, it must be a linear combination of $\mathbf{B}$ and $\mathbf{C}$.   We there-fore simplify (89) by factoring the right member so that it is exhibited as a linear combination of $\mathbf{B}$ and $\mathbf{C}$.   Thus

$$\mathbf{A} \times (\mathbf{B} \times \mathbf{C}) = (a_1 c_1 + a_2 c_2)b_1\mathbf{i} - a_1 b_1(c_1\mathbf{i} + c_2\mathbf{j}).$$

Finally, we have

$$\mathbf{A} \times (\mathbf{B} \times \mathbf{C}) = (\mathbf{A} \cdot \mathbf{C})\mathbf{B} - (\mathbf{A} \cdot \mathbf{B})\mathbf{C}, \quad (90)$$

an expansion of the triple cross product in elementary terms.

By using Theorem 8 and (90), the reader can easily show that the triple cross product $(\mathbf{A} \times \mathbf{B}) \times \mathbf{C}$ has the expansion

$$(\mathbf{A} \times \mathbf{B}) \times \mathbf{C} = (\mathbf{A} \cdot \mathbf{C})\mathbf{B} - (\mathbf{B} \cdot \mathbf{C})\mathbf{A}.$$

EXAMPLE 45.   Given $\mathbf{A} = 2\mathbf{i} - 3\mathbf{j} + \mathbf{k}$, $\mathbf{B} = \mathbf{i} - \mathbf{j}$, and $\mathbf{C} = -4\mathbf{i} + \mathbf{k}$, we compute $\mathbf{A} \times (\mathbf{B} \times \mathbf{C})$ and $(\mathbf{A} \times \mathbf{B}) \times \mathbf{C}$.

$$\begin{aligned} \mathbf{A} \times (\mathbf{B} \times \mathbf{C}) &= (\mathbf{A} \cdot \mathbf{C})\mathbf{B} - (\mathbf{A} \cdot \mathbf{B})\mathbf{C} \\ &= (-8 - 3)(\mathbf{i} - \mathbf{j}) - (2 + 3)(-4\mathbf{i} + \mathbf{k}) \\ &= -11\mathbf{i} + 11\mathbf{j} + 20\mathbf{i} - 5\mathbf{k} \\ &= 9\mathbf{i} + 11\mathbf{j} - 5\mathbf{k} \end{aligned}$$

$$\begin{aligned} (\mathbf{A} \times \mathbf{B}) \times \mathbf{C} &= (\mathbf{A} \cdot \mathbf{C})\mathbf{B} - (\mathbf{B} \cdot \mathbf{C})\mathbf{A} \\ &= -11\mathbf{i} + 11\mathbf{j} - (-4)(2\mathbf{i} - 3\mathbf{j} + \mathbf{k}) \\ &= -3\mathbf{i} - \mathbf{j} + 4\mathbf{k}. \end{aligned}$$

EXERCISES

1. Verify that $(\mathbf{A} \times \mathbf{B}) \times \mathbf{C} = (\mathbf{A} \cdot \mathbf{C})\mathbf{B} - (\mathbf{B} \cdot \mathbf{C})\mathbf{A}$.

2. If $\mathbf{A}$, $\mathbf{B}$, and $\mathbf{C}$ are given as in Example 45, compute
$$(\mathbf{B} \times \mathbf{C}) \times \mathbf{A} \text{ and } \mathbf{B} \times (\mathbf{C} \times \mathbf{A}).$$

3. Prove the identities:

$$(\mathbf{A} \times \mathbf{B}) \times (\mathbf{C} \times \mathbf{D}) = (\mathbf{A} \times \mathbf{B} \cdot \mathbf{D})\mathbf{C} - (\mathbf{A} \times \mathbf{B} \cdot \mathbf{C})\mathbf{D} \quad (91)$$

and

$$(\mathbf{A} \times \mathbf{B}) \cdot (\mathbf{C} \times \mathbf{D}) = (\mathbf{A} \cdot \mathbf{C})(\mathbf{B} \cdot \mathbf{D}) - (\mathbf{A} \cdot \mathbf{D})(\mathbf{B} \cdot \mathbf{C}) \quad (92)$$

4. By making use of (91), show that $(\mathbf{A} \times \mathbf{B}) \times (\mathbf{A} \times \mathbf{C}) = (\mathbf{A} \cdot \mathbf{B} \times \mathbf{C})\mathbf{A}$.

5. Prove Lagrange's identity:

$$(a_2b_3 - a_3b_2)^2 + (a_3b_1 - a_1b_3)^2 + (a_1b_2 - a_2b_1)^2$$
$$= (a_1{}^2 + a_2{}^2 + a_3{}^2)(b_1{}^2 + b_2{}^2 + b_3{}^2) - (a_1b_1 + a_2b_2 + a_3b_3)^2.$$

(*Hint.* Use (92), which is, indeed, sometimes referred to as the *Generalized Identity of Lagrange*.)

6. If $\mathbf{A}$, $\mathbf{B}$, $\mathbf{C}$, and $\mathbf{D}$ are coplanar, prove that

$$(\mathbf{A} \times \mathbf{B}) \times (\mathbf{C} \times \mathbf{D}) = \mathbf{O}.$$

6
trigonometry

This short chapter is devoted to illustrating the application of vector notions to the development of standard formulas of plane and spherical trigonometry. We shall see that spherical trigonometry, particularly, admits to a simple analysis in terms of vectors.

34. PLANE TRIGONOMETRY

Law of cosines. Consider the triangle of Figure 80, where $|\mathbf{A}| = a$, $|\mathbf{B}| = b$, and $|\mathbf{C}| = c$. It is clear that

$$\mathbf{C} = \mathbf{B} - \mathbf{A},$$

and that

$$\mathbf{C} \cdot \mathbf{C} = (\mathbf{B} - \mathbf{A}) \cdot (\mathbf{B} - \mathbf{A})$$

gives

$$c^2 = a^2 + b^2 - 2\mathbf{A} \cdot \mathbf{B}.$$

When we expand the last dot product, we get the familiar law of cosines

$$c^2 = a^2 + b^2 - 2ab \cos \gamma \qquad (93)$$

Law of sines. Here we seek a relation involving the

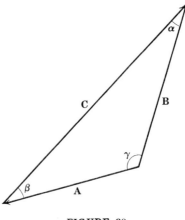

FIGURE 80

sides of the triangle of Figure 80, and the sines of its angles.   We therefore employ the cross product

$$\mathbf{C} \times \mathbf{C} = \mathbf{C} \times (\mathbf{B} - \mathbf{A}),$$

which implies

$$\mathbf{O} = \mathbf{C} \times \mathbf{B} - \mathbf{C} \times \mathbf{A},$$

or

$$\mathbf{C} \times \mathbf{A} = \mathbf{C} \times \mathbf{B}. \tag{94}$$

Equating the magnitudes of left and right members of (94) yields

$$ca \sin \beta = cb \sin \alpha,$$

which is equivalent to the *law of sines*

$$\frac{a}{\sin \alpha} = \frac{b}{\sin \beta}.$$

By repeated application, or simply by the symmetry of the variables, we have the complete relationship

$$\frac{c}{\sin \alpha} = \frac{b}{\sin \beta} = \frac{c}{\sin \gamma}, \tag{95}$$

which states that the sides of a triangle are proportional to the sines of their respective opposite angles.

Sum and difference formulas. The usual treatment of sum and difference formulas in high school textbooks requires somewhat messy geometric arguments that are further complicated by the need to consider several cases, depending on the quadrants in which the angles lie. Once again matters are greatly simplified by vectors, by means of which all cases are treated simultaneously.

Let Q and R be points on the unit circle (i.e., on a circle of radius one centered at the origin) as shown in Figure 81, so that

$$\mathbf{Q} = \cos \beta \mathbf{i} + \sin \beta \mathbf{j}$$

$$\mathbf{R} = \cos \alpha \mathbf{i} + \sin \alpha \mathbf{j}.$$

Then, $\quad \mathbf{Q} \cdot \mathbf{R} = |\mathbf{Q}|\, |\mathbf{R}| \cos (\alpha - \beta).$

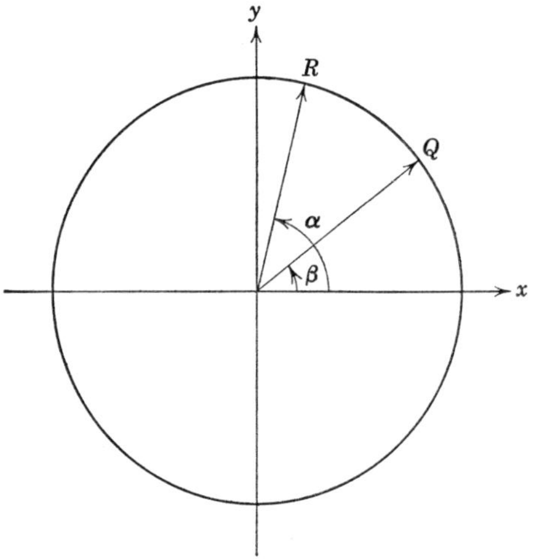

FIGURE 81

Hence

$$\cos (\alpha - \beta) = \cos \alpha \cos \beta + \sin \alpha \sin \beta. \qquad (96)$$

Once again, referring to Figure 81, we may write

$$\mathbf{Q} \times \mathbf{R} = |\mathbf{Q}| \, |\mathbf{R}| \sin (\alpha - \beta)\mathbf{k} = \sin (\alpha - \beta)\mathbf{k}.$$

In terms of coordinates this cross product becomes

$$\begin{vmatrix} \mathbf{i} & \mathbf{j} & \mathbf{k} \\ \cos \beta & \sin \beta & 0 \\ \cos \alpha & \sin \alpha & 0 \end{vmatrix} = (\sin \alpha \cos \beta - \sin \beta \cos \alpha)\mathbf{k}.$$

Thus $\sin (\alpha - \beta)\mathbf{k} = (\sin \alpha \cos \beta - \sin \beta \cos \alpha)\mathbf{k}$, which implies

$$\sin (\alpha - \beta) = \sin \alpha \cos \beta - \sin \beta \cos \alpha. \qquad (97)$$

EXERCISES

1. Using (96) and (97), deduce formulas for $\cos (\alpha + \beta)$, $\sin (\alpha + \beta)$, $\cos 2\alpha$, $\sin 2\alpha$.

2. By using vector methods, derive directly the same formulas as requested in Exercise 1.

3. Observe what happens if $\beta - \alpha$ is chosen for the expansions (96) and (97). Is the result consistent with the facts $\cos \theta = \cos (-\theta)$ and $\sin \theta = -\sin (-\theta)$ for all angles θ?

Area. The familiar formula for the area K of the triangle of Figure 80 in terms of two sides and the included angle is an immediate consequence of cross products, for

$$K = \tfrac{1}{2}|\mathbf{A} \times \mathbf{B}| = \tfrac{1}{2}|\mathbf{A}| \, |\mathbf{B}| \sin \gamma.$$

Hence $\qquad\qquad K = \tfrac{1}{2}ab \sin \gamma.$

Since a triangle is completely determined by its three sides, its area must therefore be completely expressible in terms of the sides. We shall now apply vector products to the determination of such a formula.

Consider once more the triangle of Figure 80. Its area K may be written $K = \frac{1}{2}|\mathbf{A} \times \mathbf{B}|$, which implies

$$2K = |\mathbf{A} \times \mathbf{B}|.$$

Using the scalar product to express the length of $\mathbf{A} \times \mathbf{B}$, we have

$$
\begin{aligned}
4K^2 &= |\mathbf{A} \times \mathbf{B}|^2 = (\mathbf{A} \times \mathbf{B}) \cdot (\mathbf{A} \times \mathbf{B}) \\
&= (\mathbf{A} \cdot \mathbf{A})(\mathbf{B} \cdot \mathbf{B}) - (\mathbf{A} \cdot \mathbf{B})^2 \quad \text{(by (92))} \\
&= a^2 b^2 - (\mathbf{A} \cdot \mathbf{B})^2 \\
&= (ab - \mathbf{A} \cdot \mathbf{B})(ab + \mathbf{A} \cdot \mathbf{B}). \quad (98)
\end{aligned}
$$

But, in the derivation of the law of cosines, we found that

$$\mathbf{A} \cdot \mathbf{B} = \frac{a^2 + b^2 - c^2}{2},$$

and substituting in (98) gives

$$4K^2 = \left(ab - \frac{a^2 + b^2 - c^2}{2}\right)\left(ab + \frac{a^2 + b^2 - c^2}{2}\right).$$

Simplifying, we get

$$
\begin{aligned}
4K^2 &= \tfrac{1}{4}(2ab - a^2 - b^2 + c^2)(2ab + a^2 + b^2 - c^2) \\
&= \tfrac{1}{4}(-a + b + c)(a - b + c)(a + b - c)(a + b + c).
\end{aligned}
$$

Calling $t = a + b + c$, we make the substitutions $t - 2a = -a + b + c$, $t - 2b = a - b + c$, and $t - 2c = a + b - c$.

Thus $\qquad 4K^2 = \tfrac{1}{4}(t - 2a)(t - 2b)(t - 2c)t, \qquad (99)$

and we observe that a greater simplification would have resulted if we were clever enough to introduce a variable half that of t. Because, if $2s = t$, that is,

$$s = \tfrac{1}{2}(a + b + c),$$

then

$$4K^2 = \tfrac{1}{4}(2s - 2a)(2s - 2b)(2s - 2c)2s.$$

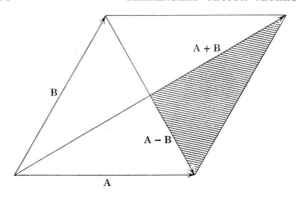

FIGURE 82

Hence $\qquad K^2 = s(s - a)(s - b)(s - c),$

and we arrive at *Hero's Formula* for the area of a triangle

$$K = \sqrt{s(s - a)(s - b)(s - c)}, \text{ where } s = \tfrac{1}{2}(a + b + c).$$

A theorem in Euclidean geometry states that *the area of a rhombus is equal to one-half the product of its diagonals.* Before giving a simple proof of this theorem, we first prove a preliminary result: *The diagonals of a rhombus are perpendicular.*

Let the sides of the rhombus be designated by **A** and **B**, as shown in Figure 82. Since all sides of a rhombus are equal, we have $|\mathbf{A}| = |\mathbf{B}|$. To determine the perpendicularity of the diagonals, we take the inner product

$$(\mathbf{A} + \mathbf{B}) \cdot (\mathbf{A} - \mathbf{B}) = |\mathbf{A}|^2 - |\mathbf{B}|^2 = 0,$$

which shows the diagonal $\mathbf{A} + \mathbf{B}$ to be perpendicular to the diagonal $\mathbf{A} - \mathbf{B}$.

Now, the area K of the rhombus is given by

$$K = 2\left|\tfrac{1}{2}(\mathbf{A} + \mathbf{B}) \times \tfrac{1}{2}(\mathbf{A} - \mathbf{B})\right|,$$

the quantity inside the absolute value signs being twice

the area of the shaded region in Figure 82. Then

$$K = \tfrac{1}{2}\left|(\mathbf{A} + \mathbf{B}) \times (\mathbf{A} - \mathbf{B})\right| = \tfrac{1}{2}\left|\mathbf{A} + \mathbf{B}\right|\,\left|\mathbf{A} - \mathbf{B}\right|\sin\frac{\pi}{2}.$$

Hence $K = \tfrac{1}{2}\left|\mathbf{A} + \mathbf{B}\right|\,\left|\mathbf{A} - \mathbf{B}\right|$, which is the desired result.

35. SPHERICAL TRIGONOMETRY

We wish to derive the basic relations involving the sides and angles of a spherical triangle. We therefore consider A, B, and C as points on a unit sphere whose center is O. Call α, β, and γ the great circle arcs[2] that form the sides of the spherical triangle ABC; α being opposite A, β being opposite B, and γ opposite C. Since the sphere is of unit radius, the arcs α, β, and γ are also the radian measures of the central angles formed by $\mathbf{B}$ and $\mathbf{C}$, $\mathbf{A}$ an $\mathbf{C}$, and $\mathbf{A}$ and $\mathbf{B}$, respectively. We further stipulate that α, β, and γ be less than π.

Amassing all the given information in terms of the vectors emanating from the center O of the sphere, we have $\mathbf{A} \cdot \mathbf{B} = \cos\gamma$, $\mathbf{B} \cdot \mathbf{C} = \cos\alpha$, and $\mathbf{A} \cdot \mathbf{C} = \cos\beta$.

As we saw earlier, the angle between two planes is determined most easily by finding the angle between perpendiculars to the planes. Thus the interior angle A between plane OAB and plane OAC is the same as the angle between $\mathbf{A} \times \mathbf{B}$ and $\mathbf{A} \times \mathbf{C}$. Since by equation 92

$$(\mathbf{A} \times \mathbf{B}) \cdot (\mathbf{A} \times \mathbf{C}) = \mathbf{B} \cdot \mathbf{C} - (\mathbf{A} \cdot \mathbf{B})(\mathbf{A} \cdot \mathbf{C}) \quad (100)$$

$$\sin\gamma \sin\beta \cos A = \cos\alpha - \cos\gamma \cos\beta, \quad (101)$$

---

[2] A *great circle* on a sphere is the intersection of the sphere with a plane through the center of the sphere. Meridian circles on the globe are all great circles, but parallels of latitude (other than the equator) are not great circles. Great circles are the so-called shortest distance paths on the surface of a sphere. Thus, if A and B are two points of a sphere, the shortest path lying on the sphere that joins A to B is along the arc of the unique (unless A and B are antipodal, or diametrically opposite, points) great circle that passes through A and B. Finally, we see that the sides of a spherical triangle are great circle arcs.

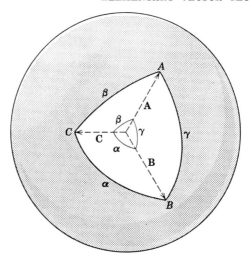

FIGURE 83

which is often termed the *law of cosines for spherical triangles.*

EXERCISE

The perpendicular vectors to two planes may intersect in an angle equal or supplementary to the angle between the given planes. Verify, by considering the direction of the perpendiculars, that the angle determined by the scalar product (100) of $\mathbf{A} \times \mathbf{B}$ and $\mathbf{A} \times \mathbf{C}$ does, in fact, yield angle A and not the supplement of A.

We shall now derive the *law of sines for spherical triangles* by first considering the expansion

$$(\mathbf{A} \times \mathbf{B}) \times (\mathbf{A} \times \mathbf{C}) = (\mathbf{A} \times \mathbf{B} \cdot \mathbf{C})\mathbf{A}. \qquad (102)$$

(See equation 91 or Exercise 4 of Section 33.)

Taking the magnitudes of both members of (102), we get

$$|\mathbf{A} \times \mathbf{B}|\, |\mathbf{A} \times \mathbf{C}|\, \sin A = |\mathbf{A} \times \mathbf{B}|\, |\cos \theta|,$$

where θ is the angle between $\mathbf{A} \times \mathbf{B}$ and $\mathbf{C}$. Thus, we have

$$|\mathbf{A} \times \mathbf{C}| \sin A = |\cos \theta|,$$

which is equivalent to

$$\sin \beta \sin A = |\cos \theta|. \tag{103}$$

Now, evaluating the magnitudes of both members of the expression

$$(\mathbf{B} \times \mathbf{A}) \times (\mathbf{B} \times \mathbf{C}) = -(\mathbf{A} \times \mathbf{B} \cdot \mathbf{C})\mathbf{B} \qquad \text{(see (91))}$$

yields

$$|\mathbf{B} \times \mathbf{A}| \, |\mathbf{B} \times \mathbf{C}| \sin B = |\mathbf{A} \times \mathbf{B}| \, |\mathbf{C}| \, |\cos \theta|,$$

which is equivalent to

$$|\mathbf{B} \times \mathbf{C}| \sin B = |\cos \theta|.$$

Simplifying, and rewriting in terms of the angles of the triangle, we have

$$\sin \alpha \sin B = |\cos \theta| \tag{104}$$

From (103) and (104) we deduce

$$\sin \alpha \sin B = \sin \beta \sin A,$$

which is the *law of sines for spherical triangles*. Again, by an interchange of letters, we may write the complete *law of sines* in the more usual form

$$\frac{\sin \alpha}{\sin A} = \frac{\sin \beta}{\sin B} = \frac{\sin \gamma}{\sin C}.$$

more geometry

We devote this chapter to a potpourri of geometric considerations.

36. LOCI DEFINED BY INEQUALITIES

In our earlier work with lines, planes, and spheres, we discussed loci that were defined by algebraic (and vector) equations. It has no doubt occurred to the reader that relations other than equality may be utilized to specify the conditions defining a locus. For example, if $\mathbf{P}$ is the position vector of a point in three-dimensional space, then $|\mathbf{P}| \leq r$ defines a locus that consists of a sphere of radius r and all points interior to the sphere, whereas $|\mathbf{P}| \geq r$ defines the locus that consists of the sphere and all points exterior to it. Analytically, these two relations would be expressed

$$x^2 + y^2 + z^2 \leq r \qquad \text{and} \qquad x^2 + y^2 + z^2 \geq r,$$

respectively. Further examples of loci so defined follow.

EXAMPLE 46. We sketch the locus defined by

$$-2x - 2 < y \leq x + 1.$$

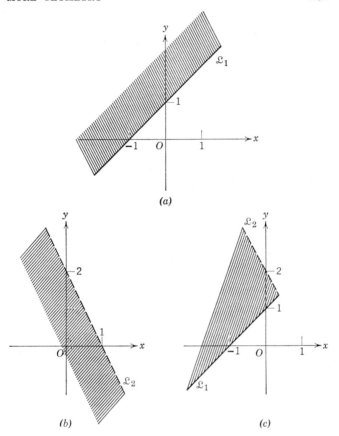

FIGURE 84

We consider, first, that $y \leq x + 1$. The *equation* $y = x + 1$ represents the familiar straight line, which is sketched in Figure 84a). Since y is larger than or equal to $x + 1$, the desired locus consists of points above the line as well as on the line itself (see Figure 84a).

The locus $-2x + 2 < y$, by similar reasoning, consists of the points below (but not including) the line $y = -2x + 2$.

(See Figure 84b. We have used a broken line to indicate that $\mathcal{L}_2$ is not included in the locus.)

The original problem imposes the two inequalities simultaneously, so the final solution may be found by combining the two sketches to determine the region of the plane that satisfies both inequalities simultaneously. This region is shaded in Figure 84c. The desired locus includes the darkened lower left portion of line $\mathcal{L}_1$ but does not include any point of $\mathcal{L}_2$. The latter is indicated by the fact that the $\mathcal{L}_2$-portion of the boundary is drawn as a broken line.

EXERCISES

1. Sketch the regions defined by the relations
   (a) $x \geq 0$ and $y \leq 0$.
   (b) $x \leq y \leq 1$.
   (c) $-2 < x < y$.
   (d) $4x - 1 < 2y \leq x + 2$.

2. What is the shape of the region $1 \leq |\mathbf{P}| \leq 2$ if
   (a) the vector $\mathbf{P}$ is a plane position vector?
   (b) the vector $\mathbf{P}$ is a position vector in three dimensions?

3. Let O be the origin of a rectangular coordinate system and P, Q any points in three dimensions such that $|\overrightarrow{OP}| = 2$ and $|\overrightarrow{PQ}| = 1$. What is the locus of Q?

4. Express analytically the fact that the points (x, y)
   (a) lie inside an annular region whose inner radius is 2 and outer radius is 3 (take the center at $(0,0)$);
   (b) lie inside triangle ABC, where $A = (1, 0)$, $B = (1, 2)$, and $C = (0, 1)$.

5. Confining attention to the x-axis, give a geometric interpretation of the points $(x, 0)$ such that
   (a) $|x - a| = b$;
   (b) $|x - a| < b$. (Assume $b \geq 0$ in both parts.)

6. What is the locus of points (x, y) such that
   (a) $|x| < 1$?
   (b) $|x| = |y|$?
   (c) $|x| \leq |y|$?
   (d) $|2x| < |y - 1|$?

(For assistance with Exercises 5 and 6, the reader is referred to Section 37c.)

37. A FEW BOOBY TRAPS

(a) How shall we sketch the plane locus defined by the equation

$$x + y = x + y?$$

At first glance it appears to be a straight line because the appearance of the equation is linear. But look once again! By grouping like terms, that is, by subtracting $x + y$ from both members, we get

$$0 = 0. \tag{105}$$

If you suggest that there is no locus, you are wrong! Let us consider the problem in the light of primary question: What ordered pairs (x, y) satisfy the relation? Clearly, any ordered pair may be substituted in (105), and the statement remains true. It is an identity, true for every choice of values for the variables. Consequently, the graph consists of the entire xy-plane.

(b) What is the locus of the parametric equations

$$x = \cos^2 t$$

$$y = \sin^2 t,$$

in which t ranges over all the real numbers?

Adding the two equations yields $x + y = 1$, which is the straight line in Figure 85a. But this cannot be the locus, for there is no value of t that yields $x = 2$ or $x = -1$! The slip-up occurred when we blithely ignored the fact that $\cos^2 t$ and $\sin^2 t$ are non-negative. The locus (see Figure 85b) is, therefore, the segment of $x + y = 1$, with the further restrictions $x \geq 0$ and $y \geq 0$, for the given parametric equations place such restriction on x and y.

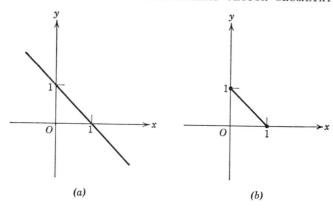

(a)   (b)

FIGURE 85

(c) What is the graph of the relation

$$|x - 1| \leq 2?$$

In order to gain geometric insight into this relation, we begin with an algebraic analysis. For which x is it true that $|x - 1| = 2$? The reader may approach this question in several ways:

(i) Using the definition of absolute value, he reasons that $x - 1 = 2$ or $x - 1 = -2$, which results in $x = 3$ or $x = -1$.

(ii) Or, he may be aware of the fact that $|a| = |b|$ if and only if $a^2 = b^2$, in which case he reduces the problem to the solution of the polynomial equation

$$(x - 1)^2 = 4,$$

which again yields $x = 3$ or $x = -1$. In either case we become aware of the fact that $|x - 1| = 2$ states that the point x (on the axis) is at a distance of two units from point 1. In general, the quantity $|x - a|$ symbolizes the distance between x and a. Thus it is reasoned that

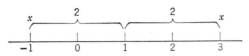

FIGURE 86

the locus $|x - 1| \leq 2$ is the segment between $x = -1$ and $x = 3$, including the endpoints. The bobby trap arises when the reader overlooks the question, "What is the dimension in which the problem has been stated?"

Hence if our discussion is of the plane, we seek the set of all (x, y) such that $|x - 1| \leq 2$. The answer now is that $-1 \leq x \leq 3$,[1] and y may be any real number, which implies a locus consisting not only of the segment on the x axis but also of the entire strip between and including the lines $x = -1$ and $x = 3$ (see Figure 87).

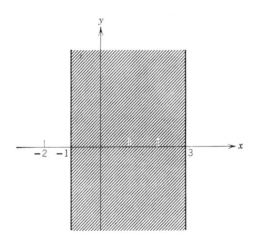

FIGURE 87

[1] In terms of set theory, we seek $\{(x, y) \mid |x - 1| \leq 2\}$, which is the same set as $\{(x, y) \mid 1 \leq x \leq 3\}$.

(*d*) What is the graph of

$$(x + y)(x - y) = 0? \tag{106}$$

Again we resort to the fundamental question: What ordered pairs (x, y) render the given relation true? We note that (106) is true if and only if

$$x + y = 0 \qquad \text{or} \qquad x - y = 0 \tag{107}$$

that is, if and only if $y = -x$ or $y = x$. Thus, the locus satisfying the given relation is a pair of lines through the origin. If point (x, y) is on either one of these lines, the relation is satisfied. (Observe that this is quite different from both relations being satisfied simultaneously; then we would have had an "and" between the equations in (107) and the locus would be the point of intersection of the two lines in the figure.)

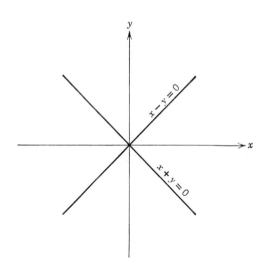

FIGURE 88

The language of set theory helps to clarify matters of this sort. Since the locus is defined with an "or," we must have the union of two sets. Therefore the locus may be written as the set

$$S = \{(x, y)\big|\ y = x\} \cup \{(x, y)\big|\ y = -x\}.$$

This description of the locus illustrates the simplicity and clarity that often result from an elementary application of the ideas of set theory.

38. SEGMENTS AND CONVEXITY

Theorem 4 provided us with a necessary and sufficient condition for a vector to have its endpoint on a line. We now turn to confining the vector endpoint to a specific segment.

Let A and B be two points and C some point of the segment AB. This situation can be described by stating that $\overrightarrow{BC} = t\overrightarrow{BA}$, where $0 \leq t \leq 1$.

In the language of position vectors relative to some fixed point O, we write

$$\begin{aligned} \mathbf{C} &= \mathbf{B} + t(\mathbf{A} - \mathbf{B}), \qquad 0 \leq t \leq 1. \\ \mathbf{C} &= t\mathbf{A} + (1 - t)\mathbf{B}. \end{aligned} \tag{108}$$

Thus the *segment* AB consists of all points that can be represented by position vectors of the form $t\mathbf{A} + (1 - t)\mathbf{B}$, where $0 \leq t \leq 1$. The endpoints occur when $t = 0$ and $t = 1$. That is,

$$\text{segment } AB = \{P\big|\mathbf{P} = t\mathbf{A} + (1 - t)\mathbf{B}\}.$$

Definition. A set is called *convex* if and only if it contains the entire line segment that joins any two points of the set. That is, a set S is said to be convex if, given any two points A and B of S, the segment AB is entirely contained in S.

EXAMPLE 47. We prove that the points of a sphere and its interior form a convex set.

Let the sphere of radius r be centered at the origin, and let A and B be any two points of the set. Then,

$$|\mathbf{A}| \leq r \qquad \text{and} \qquad |\mathbf{B}| \leq r.$$

We must show that any point of the segment AB is also a distance of less than or equal to r from the origin. The series of inequalities

$$|t\mathbf{A} + (1 - t)\mathbf{B}| \leq |t\mathbf{A}| + |(1 - t)\mathbf{B}|$$
$$= t|\mathbf{A}| + (1 - t)|\mathbf{B}| \leq tr + (1 - t)r = r$$

establishes the desired result.

EXAMPLE 48. We continue the consequences of our ability to write segments in vector language by finding an algebraic condition that a point lie interior to, or on the boundary of, a triangle.

Let A, B, and C be three distinct points not on one line. We assume, for the purposes of illustration, that a triangle (see Figure 89) consists of the points of all the segments CD, where D may be any point of segment AB. Again, using

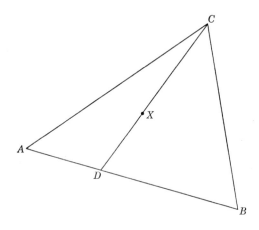

FIGURE 89

position vectors to represent points under consideration, we represent any point D of segment AB by the equation

$$\mathbf{D} = t\mathbf{A} + (1 - t)\mathbf{B}, \qquad \text{where } 0 \leq t \leq 1.$$

Thus, if X is any point of the triangle, there is some D so that X is on the segment CD, and we may write

$$\mathbf{X} = m\mathbf{C} + (1 - m)\mathbf{D}, \qquad \text{where } 0 \leq m \leq 1.$$

Then

$$\mathbf{X} = m\mathbf{C} + (1 - m)[t\mathbf{A} + (1 - t)\mathbf{B}]$$

$$= (1 - m)t\mathbf{A} + (1 - m)(1 - t)\mathbf{B} + m\mathbf{C}.$$

Noting that $(1 - m)t + (1 - m)(1 - t) + m = 1$, we draw the

Conclusion. If X is any point of the interior or boundary of triangle ABC, there are scalars r, s, and t so that $\mathbf{X} = r\mathbf{A} + s\mathbf{B} + t\mathbf{C}$, in which $\begin{cases} r + s + t = 1, \\ 0 \leq r \leq 1, \\ 0 \leq s \leq 1, \\ 0 \leq t \leq 1. \end{cases}$

EXERCISES

1. Justify each step of the series of inequalities in Example 47.

2. Graph the loci
   (a) $x^2 - y^2 = 0$
   (b) $(x^2 + y^2 - 1)(x^2 + y^2 - 2) = 0$
   (c) $(x + 2y + 1)(-x + y + 2) = 0$

3. Prove that all spheres—not only those centered at the origin —are convex.

4. Represent the points of a tetrahedron and of a square in a manner similar to the one exhibited in Example 48.

5. What condition on the coefficients of $\mathbf{A}$, $\mathbf{B}$, and $\mathbf{C}$ would guarantee that a point would be on the boundary of triangle ABC?

6. State and prove the converse of the conclusion of Example 48.

7. One might expect that the relation between $\mathbf{X}$, $\mathbf{A}$, $\mathbf{B}$, and $\mathbf{C}$ of Example 48 would depend somehow on the location of the auxiliary point (the origin of the position vectors). However,

the result of the example indicates otherwise. Can you explain why the relation between the four vectors is independent of the auxiliary point? (*Hint.* Consider the meaning of $r + s + t = 1$.)

8. What modification, if any, should be made to the result of Example 48 when the position vectors all emanate from A? That is, when $\mathbf{A} = \mathbf{O}$.

9. Let triangle ABC be defined by its vertices as follows:
$$A = (1, 0), \quad B = (1, 1), \quad \text{and } C = (0, 1)$$

(*a*) Find the median point M (point of intersection of the medians), and write its position vector in the form
$$\mathbf{M} = r\mathbf{A} + s\mathbf{B} + t\mathbf{C}.$$

(*b*) Let $r = \frac{1}{2}$, $s = \frac{1}{3}$, and $t = \frac{1}{6}$. Check the result of Example 46 by locating the point associated with these values of the coefficients.

(*c*) Find the point of intersection of the altitudes of ABC, and determine whether it is inside, outside, or on the boundary of the triangle.

10. Let tetrahedron $ABCD$ be defined by its vertices as follows:
$A = (0, 0, 0), \quad B = (1, 0, 0), \quad C = (0, 1, 0)$ and
$$D = (0, 0, 1).$$

(*a*) Write an expression, stipulating necessary conditions, for point X to be on the face ABC of the tetrahedron.

(*b*) Do likewise for X to be on the face BCD.

(*c*) How would you guarantee that X be inside (not on the boundary) of the given tetrahedron?

39. LINEAR PROGRAMMING

Consider the following problem.[2]

A hospital is concerned with minimizing the cost of its meat (beef and pork) diet. The average hospital diet

[2] This problem was suggested by a Jack Spratt problem in "Linear Programming Problems for First-Year Algebra" by Donovan Lichtenberg and Marilyn Zweng, published in *The Mathematics Teacher*, March 1960. This fine article is recommended to the reader who is interested in the details of a successful experience in the teaching of linear programming to high school students.

requires 2 pounds of lean meat and 1.5 pounds of fat meat per person per week. The beef, which costs $1.00 per pound is 0.2 fat and 0.8 lean. The pork, which costs $.75 per pound is 0.6 fat and 0.4 lean. If the hospital has 200 patients on this diet, and if it cannot purchase more than 900 pounds of meat per week because of refrigerator space, find out how many pounds of beef and how many pounds of pork should be purchased so that the cost is at a minimum.

This problem is typical of the elementary problems of *linear programming*. The word *linear* is used because the relations involving the variables will be linear relations as we shall soon see. The word *programming* stems from the fact that we are trying to determine a *program* for optimum operations. Here the hospital seeks a *program* (for the purchasing of meats) which is optimum in the sense that it would satisfy the needs of the hospital while minimizing the cost.

Let's extract the pertinent data from the hospital problem. Let

B = pounds of beef to purchase each week, and

P = pounds of pork to purchase each week.

It is clear that

$$B \geq 0 \qquad \text{and} \qquad P \geq 0. \qquad (a)$$

The restriction of refrigerator space tells us that

$$B + P \leq 900. \qquad (b)$$

The rest of the given data can be summarized in the table

	Fat	Lean	Cost/lb
Beef	0.2	0.8	$1.00
Pork	0.6	0.4	0.75

Since a total of $200 \cdot 2 = 400$ pounds of lean meat is required, we see that

$$0.8B + 4P \geq 400; \qquad (c)$$

and since a total of $200 \cdot 1.5 = 300$ pounds of fat meat is required, we have

$$0.2B + 0.6P \geq 300. \qquad (d)$$

Finally, we write an expression for the cost C (in dollars) of the purchase

$$C(B, P) = B + \tfrac{3}{4}P. \qquad (e)$$

In accordance with the earlier prediction, all the relations involving B and P are linear relations. The inequalities $(a) - (d)$ place restrictions on B and P. Our problem, then, is to select the ordered pair (B, P) that yields a minimum value for $C(B, P)$, provided (a)–(d) hold. Thus we turn our attention to finding, graphically, the set R of ordered pairs (B, P) that satisfy the given restrictions. This set is

$$R = \{(B, P) | B \geq 0, P \geq 0, B + P \leq 900,$$
$$2B + P \geq 1000, B + 3P \geq 1500\}.$$

The set R is the darkest region shown in Figure 90. We have thus narrowed the choice of ordered pairs to those of the triangle R, but we still have an infinite number of choices—certainly too many for a trial and error procedure unless we were willing to settle for an approximate answer. Fortunately, however, there is a theorem to assist us in narrowing the search considerably.

Theorem 12. *Let f be a linear function whose domain of definition is a convex polygon. The minimum value of $f(x, y)$ is attained at a vertex of the polygon.* (The

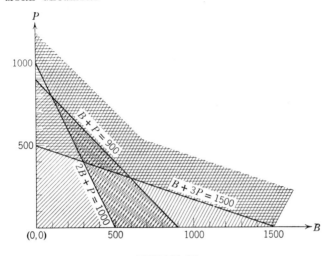

FIGURE 90

word "maximum" may be substituted for "minimum," without disturbing the validity of the theorem.)

Returning to the original problem, we determine the vertices of R as: $S = (100,800)$, $T = (600,300)$, and $U = (300,400)$. Applying Theorem 12, which has narrowed our search to the points S, T, and U, we evaluate

$$C(100,800) = 1 \cdot 100 + \frac{3}{4} \cdot 800 = \$700$$

$$C(600,300) = 1 \cdot 600 + \frac{3}{4} \cdot 300 = \$825$$

$$C(300,400) = 1 \cdot 300 + \frac{3}{4} \cdot 400 = \$600,$$

giving the conclusion that 300 pounds of beef and 400 pounds of pork make up the optimum purchasing program for the hospital.

Proof of Theorem 12. Let the value of the linear[3] function at $P = (x, y)$ be given by

$$f(x, y) = ax + by + c.$$

We first consider the values of $f(x, y)$ when P is confined to the segment P_1P_2, where $P_1 = (x_1, y_1)$ and $P_2(x_2, y_2)$. We show that, under this restriction, the maximum and minimum values of $f(x, y)$ are attained at the end-points of the segment.

In Section 38 we learned that if $P = (x, y)$ belongs to the segment P_1P_2, then

$$x = lx_1 + (1 - l)x_2 = x_2 + l(x_1 - x_2),$$

$$y = ly_1 + (1 - l)y_2 = y_2 + l(y_1 - y_2),$$

in which $0 \leq l \leq 1$. Then the value of f at P is

$$\begin{aligned}
f(x, y) &= a[x_2 + l(x_1 - x_2)] + b[y_2 + l(y_1 - y_2)] + c \\
&= ax_2 + by_2 + l(ax_1 - ax_2 + by_1 - by_2) + c \\
&= (ax_2 + by_2 + c) + l[(ax_1 + by_1 + c) \\
&\qquad\qquad\qquad\qquad - (ax_2 + by_2 + c)] \\
&= f(x_2, y_2) + l[f(x_1\, y_1) - f(x_2, y_2)].
\end{aligned}$$

Hence $f(x, y)$ ranges between $f(x_1, y_1)$ and $f(x_2, y_2)$ as $0 \leq l \leq 1$. The extreme (maximum and minimum) values of the function are attained at the endpoints of the segment.

Query. What happens if $f(x_1, y_1) = f(x_2, y_2)$? Examine the proof to see if your answer is substantiated.

The remainder of the proof for Theorem 12 is left as an exercise for the reader, with the hint that the definitions of *polygon* and *convexity* are essential.

---

[3] Strictly speaking, this function is linear if and only if $c = 0$. Since the term "linear" is often used in a loose manner to include expressions of the form $ax + by + c$, when $c \neq 0$, we have chosen to exhibit a proof of Theorem 12 for such a loose interpretation of "linear."

ADDITIONAL EXERCISE

Make the following replacements in the statement of Theorem 12:

> "polyhedron" for "polygon," and
> "$f(x, y, z)$" for "$f(x, y)$."

Prove the resulting statement.

EXAMPLE 49. A moving van company charges 25 cents per pound for moving furniture from New York to San Francisco and 15 cents per pound for moving crates on the same cross-country trip. If at least one quarter of each load is furniture and at least one quarter of each load consists of crates, find the minimum and maximum cost per pound for a load.

Let F = that fraction of a load that is furniture,

C = that fraction of a load that consists of crates.

Then
$$\frac{1}{4} \le F \le \frac{3}{4},$$

and
$$\frac{1}{4} \le C \le \frac{3}{4}.$$

Furthermore, since a load consists entirely of furniture and crates, we have the additional relation

$$F + C = 1.$$

These three relations define a *segment*, as shown in Figure 91. Our problem reduces to a consideration of cost on a one-dimensional set, a segment whose endpoints are $(\frac{1}{4}, \frac{3}{4})$ and $(\frac{3}{4}, \frac{1}{4})$.

The cost $K(F, C)$ is given by the relation $K(F, C) = .25F + .15C$.

$$K\left(\frac{1}{4}, \frac{3}{4}\right) = 0.25\left(\frac{1}{4}\right) + 0.15\left(\frac{3}{4}\right) = \frac{0.70}{4} = 0.175$$

$$K\left(\frac{3}{4}, \frac{1}{4}\right) = 0.25\left(\frac{3}{4}\right) + 0.15\left(\frac{1}{4}\right) = \frac{0.90}{4} = 0.225.$$

Hence, the minimum cost for a load would be $17\frac{1}{2}$ cents per pound, while the maximum would be $22\frac{1}{2}$ cents per pound.

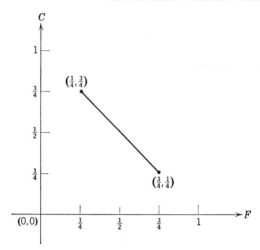

FIGURE 91

EXAMPLE 50. A sporting goods company makes baseball bats and softball bats, which are processed first by a lathe that cuts the wood to size and then by a finishing machine that paints, dries, polishes, and labels the bats. The lathe operates 6 minutes to produce a baseball bat and 3 minutes to produce a softball bat. The finishing machine operates for 3 minutes on a bat, no matter which kind. However, because of loading and maintenance problems, the lathe can operate only 4 hours per day and the finishing machine can operate only 3 hours per day. If the profit on a baseball bat is $1.00 and the profit on a softball bat 75 cents, and if the company can sell all the bats it makes, find how many of each kind it should produce daily in order to realize maximum profit.

Although there seems to be a mass of detail, the problem can be summarized easily in the following manner. Let

$b =$ the number of baseball bats produced daily,

$s =$ the number of softball bats produced daily.

The restriction $(4 \cdot 60$ minutes per day) on the lathe operation gives

$$6b + 3s \leq 240 \quad \text{or} \quad 2b + s \leq 80. \tag{a}$$

The restriction (3 · 60 minutes per day) on the finishing machine gives

$$3b + 3s \leq 180 \qquad \text{or} \qquad b + s \leq 60. \qquad (b)$$

We know also that

$$b \geq 0. \qquad (c)$$

$$s \geq 0. \qquad (d)$$

The profit $P(b, s)$ per day would be

$$P(b, s) = b + \tfrac{3}{4}s. \qquad (e)$$

Thus all the data are summarized in terms of inequalities (a)–(d) and the relation (e). We seek to maximize $P(b, s)$ on the convex polygon determined by the restrictions (a)–(d). The polygon is exhibited in Figure 92. The vertices of the polygon are

$$O = (0, 0), \quad A = (40, 0), \quad B = (20, 40), \quad \text{and } C = (0, 60).$$

Evaluating the profit at these four points shows that a maximum would be achieved by the production of softball bats only.

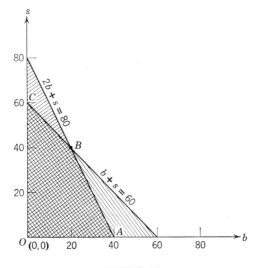

FIGURE 92

EXAMPLE 51. A chocolate manufacturing concern makes milk chocolate, semisweet chocolate, and bitter chocolate. It can produce 500 pounds per day, but demand for the various types is such that the maximum amounts that can be sold are as follows

milk—400 pounds per day
semisweet—300 pounds per day
bitter—200 pounds per day.

If the profit is 80 cents per pound for bitter, 75 cents per pound for semi-sweet, and 60 cents per pound for milk chocolate, determine the program for production that would maximize the profit.

Although this problem could be handled by only two variables, we shall treat it as a three-dimensional problem for purposes of illustration. Let

m = pounds of milk chocolate produced per day

s = pounds of semisweet chocolate produced per day

b = pounds of bitter chocolate produced per day.

Then

$$m + s + b \le 500 \qquad (a)$$

$$0 \le m \le 400 \qquad (b)$$

$$0 \le s \le 300 \qquad (c)$$

$$0 \le b \le 200. \qquad (d)$$

The profit function P is defined by the relation $P(m, s, b) = \frac{3}{5}m + \frac{3}{4}s + \frac{4}{5}b$ (in dollars).

The graph of restrictions (a)–(d) is shown in Figure 93. An algebraic solution for the vertices of the polyhedron shows

$A = (400, 0, 100), \quad B = (400, 0, 0), \quad C = (400, 100, 0),$

$D = (200, 300, 0), \quad E = (0, 300, 200), \quad F = (0, 0, 200),$

and $\qquad\qquad\qquad G = (300, 0, 200).$

We may conclude that the concern would achieve a maximum profit by producing only two types or one type of chocolate. The latter alternative is excluded because producing less than 500 pounds would always result in a loss. We may therefore conclude that two kinds of chocolate should be manufactured. So the search is confined to an investigation of the profit at

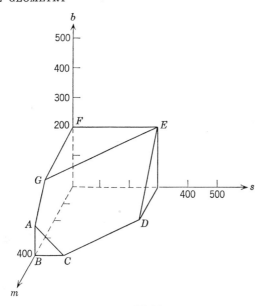

FIGURE 93

points A, C, D, E, and G—the points of a plane represented by $m + s + b = 500$.

The computation of profit at these vertices is left as an exercise for the reader.

EXERCISES

1. (*a*) Carry out Example 51 as a two variable problem.

(*b*) Carry out Example 51 with the restriction that the maximum amount of bitter chocolate that can be sold is 100 pounds per day.

2. Find the minimum and maximum values of $f(x, y) = 2x + 4y - 1$ on the set defined by the inequalities

$$-2x + 3y \leq 6$$

$$x + y \leq 2$$

$$x + 2y \geq 3.$$

3. The delivery trucks owned by an oil company have a capacity of 1000 gallons. On each trip a truck must carry at least 400 gallons of regular gasoline, at least 200 gallons of high test gasoline, and, at most, 300 gallons of white gasoline. If the profit per gallon is 3 cents for regular, 4 cents for high test, and 5 cents for white gas, find the program for loading the trucks that would yield a maximum profit. (This can be done with only two variables.)

4. Assume the trucks in Exercise 3 are all loaded to capacity. What kind of loading would yield the least profit?

5. A mountain climbing party wishes to purchase A-rations and B-rations for an expedition. The food values and costs per unit are classified as follows:

	A	B
Units of carbohydrate	1	3
Units of protein	3	4
Units of fat	3	1
Cost	\$2	\$1

The minimum requirements are 10 carbohydrate units, 18 protein units, and 6 fat units. Find the minimum cost diet satisfying the requirements of the mountain climbers.

(Observe that the convex region is not a closed polygon in this case. How do you know that you have the minimum?)

40. THEOREMS ARISING IN MORE GENERAL GEOMETRIES

The study of projective geometry deals with some of the same entities discussed in Euclidean geometry, namely points, lines, and planes. However, projective geometry discards the notions of distance and angle measurements, and focuses attention on *incidence properties:* points lying on lines, lines passing through points, intersections of various sorts, and so forth. For elementary discussions of *projective geometry*, the reader is referred to Chapter IV of *What is Mathematics?* by

Courant and Robbins, and to the *Real Projective Plane* by H. S. M. Coxeter. We shall look into two of the principal results of this field of study: the theorems of *Desargues* and *Pappus*.

Desargues' theorem.   *If two triangles have corresponding vertices joined by concurrent lines, then the intersections of corresponding sides are collinear* (see Figure 94).

The reader should observe that the theorem is devoid of metric concepts.   It is concerned with neither lengths of sides nor with the size of the angles of the triangle.

One of the axioms of projective geometry states that every two lines intersect, that is, parallelism is ruled out. Consequently, the intersections referred to in Desargues' theorem, namely points P, Q, and R, must exist in projective geometry.   But, if we consider the hypothesis of Desargues' theorem in Euclidean geometry, parallelism may interfere with the existence of P, Q, and R.   We therefore precede the generalized projective version of

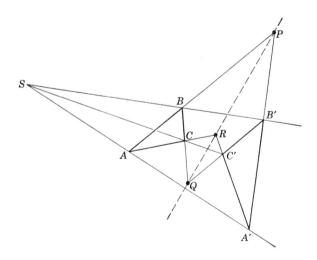

FIGURE 94

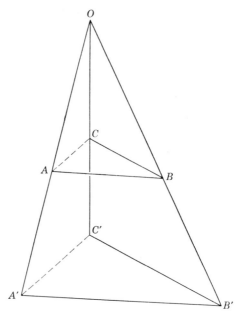

FIGURE 95

Desargues' theorem with a special case that arises in Euclidean geometry.

Theorem D. *Let ABC and A'B'C' be two triangles with AB parallel to A'B' and BC parallel to B'C' while lines AA', BB', and CC' meet in O. Then AC is parallel to A'C'.*

In terms of our standard use of position vectors emanating from O, we have the following collinearities: O, C, and C'; O, A, and A'; O, B, and B'. These imply respectively: $\mathbf{A} = r\mathbf{A}'$, $\mathbf{B} = s\mathbf{B}'$ and $\mathbf{C} = t\mathbf{C}'$. And AB parallel to $A'B'$ implies $\mathbf{B} - \mathbf{A} = l(\mathbf{B}' - \mathbf{A}')$. But $\mathbf{B} - \mathbf{A} = s\mathbf{B}' - r\mathbf{A}'$. Hence, $r = s = l$. Similarly,

$$\mathbf{C} - \mathbf{B} = m(\mathbf{C}' - \mathbf{B}') = t\mathbf{C}' - s\mathbf{B}',$$

which implies $s = t = m$.   Combining these results, we have $l = m = r = s = t$.   Now,

$$\mathbf{C} - \mathbf{A} = t\mathbf{C}' - r\mathbf{A}' = r(\mathbf{C}' - \mathbf{A}'),$$

which states that AC is parallel to $A'C'$, the result we set out to prove.   (Note that the given triangles may or may not be in the same plane.   The vector proof is valid in both cases.)

Under the assumption that every two lines meet, we present a vector proof of general form of Desargues' theorem.

As in Figure 94, let the two triangles be ABC and $A'B'C'$ with the corresponding vertices joined by concurrent lines meeting at S.   Call P, Q, and R the intersections of corresponding sides, as follows:

P the intersection of AB and $A'B'$

Q the intersection of BC and $B'C'$, and

R the intersection of CA and $C'A'$.

Again we use position vectors emanating from some point O (which does not appear in the figure).

The fact that S is collinear with every pair of corresponding vertices allows us to write

$$\mathbf{S} = r\mathbf{A} + (1 - r)\mathbf{A}' = s\mathbf{B} + (1 - s)\mathbf{B}'$$
$$= t\mathbf{C} + (1 - t)\mathbf{C}'.$$

This triple equality implies the following three relations:

$$r\mathbf{A} - s\mathbf{B} = (1 - s)\mathbf{B}' - (1 - r)\mathbf{A}'$$
$$s\mathbf{B} - t\mathbf{C} = (1 - t)\mathbf{C}' - (1 - s)\mathbf{B}'$$
$$t\mathbf{C} - r\mathbf{A} = (1 - r)\mathbf{A}' - (1 - t)\mathbf{C}'.$$

Noting that the sum of the coefficients of left and right members in each of these three equations is equal, we have the opportunity to use Theorem 4, by dividing and having the sum of the coefficients equal to 1.

$$\frac{r}{r-s}\mathbf{A} - \frac{s}{r-s}\mathbf{B} = \frac{1-s}{r-s}\mathbf{B}' - \frac{1-r}{r-s}\mathbf{A}'. \quad (109)$$

$$\frac{s}{s-t}\mathbf{B} - \frac{t}{s-t}\mathbf{C} = \frac{1-t}{s-t}\mathbf{C}' - \frac{1-s}{s-t}\mathbf{B}'. \quad (110)$$

$$\frac{t}{t-r}\mathbf{C} - \frac{r}{t-r}\mathbf{A} = \frac{1-r}{t-r}\mathbf{A}' - \frac{1-t}{t-r}\mathbf{C}'. \quad (111)$$

Each member of (109) represents a vector emanating from O, with its endpoint on $A'B'$ and on AB, simultaneously. This vector is $\mathbf{P}$. That is,

$$\mathbf{P} = \frac{r}{r-s}\mathbf{A} - \frac{s}{r-s}\mathbf{B}$$

or
$$(r-s)\mathbf{P} = r\mathbf{A} - s\mathbf{B}. \quad (112)$$

Similar reasoning with (110) and (111) yields

$$(s-t)\mathbf{Q} = s\mathbf{B} - t\mathbf{C} \quad (113)$$

and

$$(t-r)\mathbf{R} = t\mathbf{C} - r\mathbf{A}. \quad (114)$$

Finally, (112), (113), and (114) give us

$$(r-s)\mathbf{P} = -(s-t)\mathbf{Q} - (t-r)\mathbf{R},$$

or
$$\mathbf{P} = \frac{t-s}{r-s}\mathbf{Q} + \frac{r-t}{r-s}\mathbf{R},$$

which establishes the collinearity of P, Q, and R, for the coefficients $t - s/r - s$ and $r - t/r - s$ sum to unity.

EXERCISE

What justification is there in performing the divisions by $r - s$, $s - t$, and $t - r$ to obtain (109), (110), and (111)? What would be implied by any of these denominators being zero?

Pappus' theorem. Pappus of Alexandria (3rd century A.D.) was the last of the remarkable Greek mathematicians of antiquity. Among his original contributions is a theorem that can be stated as *a pure incidence theorem*, devoid of metric concepts, and therefore falling into the category of *projective theorems.*

If alternate vertices of a plane hexagon lie on two lines, the three pairs of opposite sides meet in three collinear points.

We may restate the theorem in specific terms as follows:

If A, B, C are distinct points of line $\mathcal{L}_1$ and A', B', C' are distinct points of another line $\mathcal{L}_2$, the three points of intersection of the pairs of lines AB' and $A'B$, and BC' and $B'C$, CA', and $C'A$ are collinear.

Before proceeding with the proof, we point out once again that every two lines are assumed to intersect in projective geometry. If one considers Pappus' theorem in the strict realm of Euclidean geometry, one must consider special cases where parallelism may arise and interfere with the existence of certain intersections (see Exercise 4, page 191).

Proof of Pappus' Theorem. Referring to Figure 96, we call **U** a unit vector along $\mathcal{L}_1$ and **V** a unit vector

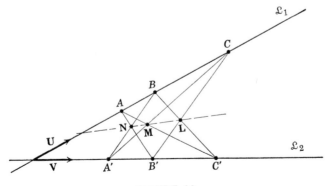

FIGURE 96

along $\mathcal{L}_2$. Thus we may write

$$\mathbf{A} = a\mathbf{U}, \quad \mathbf{B} = b\mathbf{U}, \quad \mathbf{C} = c\mathbf{U},$$

and $$\mathbf{A}' = a'\mathbf{V}, \quad \mathbf{B}' = b'\mathbf{V}, \quad \mathbf{C}' = c'\mathbf{V}.$$

Since L is collinear with B and C', we may invoke Theorem 4 to write

$$\mathbf{L} = l\mathbf{B} + (1 - l)\mathbf{C}' = lb\mathbf{U} + (1 - l)c'\mathbf{V}.$$

And since L is also collinear with B' and C, we may also write

$$\mathbf{L} = \lambda\mathbf{C} + (1 - \lambda)\mathbf{B}' = \lambda c\mathbf{U} + (1 - \lambda)b'\mathbf{V}.$$

These two representations imply

$$lb = \lambda c$$
$$(1 - l)c' = (1 - \lambda)b',$$

which solving for l and λ, yields

$$l = \frac{b'c - cc'}{bb' - cc'} \quad \text{and} \quad \lambda = \frac{bb' - bc'}{bb' - cc'}.$$

Thus

$$\mathbf{L} = \frac{bc(b' - c')}{bb' - cc'}\,\mathbf{U} + \frac{b'c'(b - c)}{bb' - cc'}\,\mathbf{V}.$$

Similarly, it can be shown that

$$\mathbf{M} = \frac{ac(c' - a')}{cc' - aa'}\,\mathbf{U} + \frac{a'c'(c - a)}{cc' - aa'}\,\mathbf{V},$$

and $$\mathbf{N} = \frac{ab(a' - b')}{aa' - bb'}\,\mathbf{U} + \frac{a'b'(a - b)}{aa' - bb'}\,\mathbf{V}.$$

To determine whether L, M, and N are collinear, we seek r, s, and t, such that

$$r\mathbf{L} + s\mathbf{M} + t\mathbf{N} = \mathbf{O}.$$

(What other algebraic relation must r, s, and t satisfy before we may conclude collinearity?)

Perseverance with elementary algebra yields the solution

$$r = aa'(bb' - cc'), \quad s = bb'(cc' - aa'),$$
$$t = cc'(aa' - bb'),$$

from which we do conclude that L, M, and N are collinear. (Now, do we know that r, s, and t are not all zero?)

The theorem we have just proved possesses mathematical significance far beyond any dreams that Pappus could have had back in the third century. Approximately one hundred years ago a method of building up number systems from geometry was first discovered by a German mathematician, Karl G. C. von Staudt. Since that time much creative work has been done on the foundations of geometry and its interrelationship with the algebraic structure of number systems that can be built up from geometry. One of the great achievements of this study is a remarkable theorem, first proved by David Hilbert (1862–1943) around the turn of the century, which states:

A number system related to a geometry satisfies the law $a \cdot b = b \cdot a$ if and only if Pappus' theorem is valid in the geometry. (The "dot" here stands for multiplication.)

The geometry we have been working with is Euclidean, and the number system for our analytic geometry is the real number system, in which multiplication is commutative, that is, $a \cdot b = b \cdot a$. Thus we were able to prove Pappus' theorem; and, conversely, if we had developed a number system with the aid of Pappus' theorem, its multiplication would necessarily be commutative.

Since it is hardly possible to enter into a detailed discussion of the foundations of geometry in this short work, we shall have to content ourselves by closing with the remark that it is a rich subject, which has resulted in the discovery of many strange number systems as well as geometries. There are geometries for which the coordinate number system has $1 + 1 \neq 2$; in fact, where $1 + 1 = 0$. There are geometries in which neither Pappus' theorem nor Desargues' theorem holds true. And stranger yet is the fact that such geometries and their accompanying number systems have found a wide variety of applications in fields as diverse as the design of agricultural and other experiments, military logistics, psychology, and the study of mathematical machines.

The theorem of Menelaus. Menelaus of Alexandria, who wrote a treatise on spheres and actually made some discoveries in spherical trigonometry in the 1st century A.D., is also noted for having discovered an interesting theorem concerning transversals.

If a transversal cuts the sides AB, BC, and CA of triangle ABC in the points L, M, and N, respectively,

$$\frac{AL}{LB} \cdot \frac{BM}{MC} \cdot \frac{CN}{NA} = -1, \qquad (115)$$

where all segments referred to are directed segments.
Conversely, if points L, M, and N are on the respective sides AB, BC, and CA or triangle ABC, and

$$\frac{AL}{LB} \cdot \frac{BM}{MC} \cdot \frac{CN}{NA} = -1,$$

then L, M, and N are collinear.

We shall prove only the first part of the theorem, leaving the converse as an exercise for the reader.

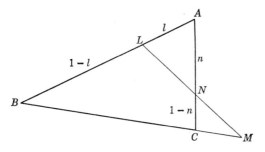

FIGURE 97

Consider all position vectors of points emanating from point A, and

> L divides AB in the ratio $l : 1 - l$
>
> M divides BC in the ratio $m : 1 - m$
>
> N divides AC in the ratio $n : 1 - n$.

These conditions state

$$\frac{AL}{LB} \cdot \frac{BM}{MC} \cdot \frac{CN}{NA} = \frac{l}{1-l} \cdot \frac{m}{1-m} \cdot \frac{1-n}{n}.$$

Then

$$\mathbf{L} = l\mathbf{B}, \quad \mathbf{N} = n\mathbf{C}, \quad \text{and} \quad \overrightarrow{BM} = m\overrightarrow{BC} = m(\mathbf{C} - \mathbf{B}). \tag{116}$$

(Figure 97 illustrates the case where $l < 1$, $n < 1$, and $m > 1$.) Therefore $\mathbf{M} - \mathbf{B} = m\mathbf{C} - m\mathbf{B}$ and

$$\mathbf{M} = (1 - m)\mathbf{B} + m\mathbf{C}. \tag{117}$$

Now, since L, M, and N are collinear, we know that there exists a real number r such that

$$\mathbf{M} = r\mathbf{L} + (1 - r)\mathbf{N}. \tag{118}$$

From (116), (117), and (118), we deduce

$$(1 - m)\mathbf{B} + m\mathbf{C} = rl\mathbf{B} + (1 - r)n\mathbf{C}.$$

Hence $m = (1 - r)n$ and $rl = 1 - m,$

which imply $l = \dfrac{1 - m}{r} = \dfrac{1 - (1 - r)n}{r}.$

We are now in a position to examine the product of the three ratios in terms of r and n alone:

$$
\begin{aligned}
\frac{l}{1 - l} \cdot \frac{m}{1 - m} \cdot \frac{1 - n}{n} &= \frac{\dfrac{1 - (1 - r)n}{r}}{1 - \dfrac{1 - (1 - r)n}{r}} \\
&\qquad \cdot \frac{(1 - r)n}{1 - (1 - r)n} \cdot \frac{1 - n}{n} \\
&= \frac{1 - (1 - r)n}{r - 1 + (1 - r)n} \\
&\qquad \cdot \frac{(1 - r)n}{1 - (1 - r)n} \cdot \frac{1 - n}{n} \\
&= \frac{(1 - r)(1 - n)}{(r - 1)(1 - n)} = -1,
\end{aligned}
$$

which is the result we wished to prove.

EXERCISES

1. Prove the converse of the Menelaus theorem.

   Hint: $\mathbf{M} = a\mathbf{L} + b\mathbf{N}$ for some scalars a and b.   Prove that $a + b = 1$, by using the relation $\dfrac{l}{1 - l} \cdot \dfrac{m}{1 - m} \cdot \dfrac{1 - n}{n} = -1.$

(You might try to eliminate one of the scalars, say l, by first solving for it in terms of m and n.)

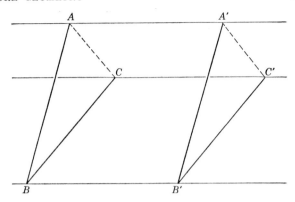

FIGURE 98

2. Prove the special Euclidean case of Desargues' theorem, which reads: Let ABC and $A'B'C'$ be two triangles with AB parallel to $A'B'$, and BC parallel to $B'C'$ while lines AA', BB', and CC' are parallel. Then AC must be parallel to $A'C'$ (see Figure 98).

3. Prove the following special case of Pappus' theorem. If two sets of three points A, B, C and A', B', C' on two coplanar lines $\mathcal{L}$ and $\mathcal{L}'$, respectively, are so related that the lines AA', BB', CC' meet in a point, the points of intersection of the pairs of lines AB' and BA', BC' and CB', CA', and AC' are collinear with the point of intersection of $\mathcal{L}$ and $\mathcal{L}'$.

4. Prove by vector methods the following special Euclidean case of Pappus' theorem: If A, B, C are distinct points of line $\mathcal{L}$ and A', B', C' are distinct points of $\mathcal{L}'$ such that AB' is parallel to BC' and $A'B$ is parallel to $B'C$, then AA' must be parallel to CC'.

Why is this a special case of Pappus' theorem?

41. APPLICATIONS OF PARAMETRIC
EQUATIONS TO LOCUS PROBLEMS

The cycloid. Consider a wheel set on a line and permitted to roll without slippage. An interesting problem,

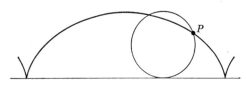

FIGURE 99

and one whose results are applicable to certain engineering problems, is the following: What is the locus of a fixed point P on the rim as the wheel rolls along the line? (See Figure 99.)

To simplify matters we allow the line to be the x-axis and let P begin at the origin of the coordinate system. We call C the center and r the radius of the wheel. The parameter θ is used to denote the angle through which the radius CP has rotated. Referring to Figure 100, the

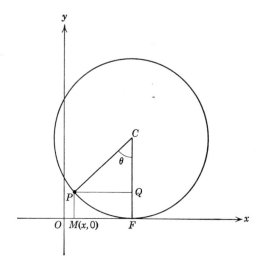

FIGURE 100

horizontal distance OF is equal to the arc $\overset{\frown}{FP}$, by the assumption that the wheel does not slip; and from trigonometry we know that $\overset{\frown}{FP} = r\theta$, where θ is measured in radians. Thus $OF = r\theta$. We shall use this important fact in determining the x- and y-coordinates of P.

$$x = OF - MF = r\theta - PQ.$$

But from triangle PCQ we see that

$$\sin \theta = \frac{PQ}{PC} = \frac{PQ}{r}.$$

Thus, $PQ = r \sin \theta$, and the x-coordinate of P is

$$x = r\theta - r \sin \theta = r(\theta - \sin \theta).$$

Again, referring to Figure 100, we note that

$$y = MP = FQ = CF - QC = r - QC;$$

but $$CQ = CP \cos \theta = r \cos \theta.$$

Hence $$y = r - r \cos \theta = r(1 - \cos \theta),$$

and we have

$$\begin{cases} x = r(\theta - \sin \theta) \\ y = r(1 - \cos \theta) \end{cases}$$

as the parametric representation of the desired locus, which is called a *cycloid*.

Involutes. We shall confine our attention to involutes of circles, for these curves are easily treated without the use of calculus. The more general theory is part of the field of differential geometry and requires—as the name suggests—differential calculus as its instrument of analysis.

Consider a string (of a mathematical or ideal sort, with zero thickness) to be tightly wound about a circular post,

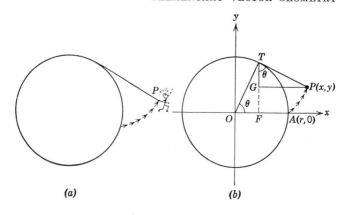

FIGURE 101

and call P the endpoint of the string. The *involute of a circle* is the curve described by point P as the string is unwound while being held taut (see Figure 101).

We shall now derive parametric equations for the involute, using the fact that the portion of the string already unwound is tangential to the circle (because it is being held taut).

Let the circle of radius r be centered at the origin, and suppose the initial position of P to be at $A = (r, 0)$ on the x-axis. We arbitrarily choose the unwinding to take place in a counter-clockwise direction, calling the unwound portion of the string PT, where OT is a radius making an angle θ with the horizontal radius OA.

Referring to triangle TGP in Figure 101b, we observe that angle GTP is equal to θ, which allows us to write

$$GP = TP \sin \theta \quad \text{and} \quad GT = TP \cos \theta. \quad (119)$$

Since the unwound string TP is equal in length to the arc $\overset{\frown}{AT}$, we have $TP = \overset{\frown}{AT} = r\theta$, which permits us to rewrite (119) in the form

$$GP = r\theta \sin \theta \quad \text{and} \quad GT = r\theta \cos \theta.$$

We are now ready to determine expressions for the coordinates of P in terms of the parameter θ.

$$x = OF + GP = r \cos \theta + r\theta \sin \theta = r(\cos \theta + \theta \sin \theta),$$

and $\quad y = FT - GT = r \sin \theta - r\theta \cos \theta$
$$= r(\sin \theta - \theta \cos \theta).$$

Thus a parametric representation of *the involute of the circle* is

$$\begin{cases} x = r(\cos \theta + \theta \sin \theta) \\ y = r(\sin \theta - \theta \cos \theta). \end{cases} \quad (120)$$

Vector methods are often of assistance in determining loci of the type just considered. We therefore attempt a derivation of (120) from the vector point of view in the hope that it may be instructive to the reader.

The position vector $\overrightarrow{OP} = x\mathbf{i} + y\mathbf{j}$
$$= \overrightarrow{OT} + \overrightarrow{TP}$$
$$= r \cos \theta\mathbf{i} + r \sin \theta\mathbf{j} + \overrightarrow{TP}.$$

We call $\overrightarrow{TP} = a\mathbf{i} + b\mathbf{j}$ and determine a and b.

$$\left|\overrightarrow{TP}\right| = \sqrt{a^2 + b^2} = r\theta, \quad (121)$$

and $\qquad \overrightarrow{TP} \cdot \overrightarrow{OT} = ar \cos \theta + br \sin \theta = 0.$

Since $r \neq 0$, we may divide by r, getting

$$a \cos \theta + b \sin \theta = 0$$

or $\qquad\qquad a = -b \tan \theta.$

Substituting this value for a in (121) yields

$$\sqrt{b^2 \tan^2 \theta + b^2} = r\theta$$

or $$b \sec \theta = r\theta,$$

which implies $$b = r\theta \cos \theta$$

and $$a = -r\theta \sin \theta.$$

Thus $$\overrightarrow{TP} = -r\theta \sin \theta \mathbf{i} + r\theta \cos \theta \mathbf{j}.$$

We are now equipped to return to the problem of getting an explicit formulation for $\overrightarrow{OP}$.

$$\overrightarrow{OP} = r \cos \theta \mathbf{i} + r \sin \theta \mathbf{j} - r\theta \sin \theta \mathbf{i} + r \cos \theta \mathbf{j}$$

$$= r(\cos \theta - \theta \sin \theta)\mathbf{i} + r(\sin \theta + \theta \cos \theta)\mathbf{j}.$$

Therefore

$$\begin{cases} x = r(\cos \theta - \theta \sin \theta) & (122) \\ y = r(\sin \theta + \theta \cos \theta), \end{cases}$$

which differs from the parametric form (120)! Why? See Exercise 1 below.

EXERCISES

1. The parametric representation (122) is in error, for some careless algebra was put forth in the argument. Find the error and give a valid vector-type derivation of the involute of a circle.

2. (a) A wheel of radius r rolls along a line without slipping. Find the locus described by a point P on a spoke of the wheel, where P is at a distance a from the center of the wheel. This curve is known as a *trochoid* or *prolate cycloid* (see Figure 102a).

(b) What is the locus if $a > r$, as is the case when P is on the rim or flange of a locomotive wheel (see figure 102b). This curve is called a *curate cycloid*. (Observe that a description of this locus shows that some part of a locomotive is moving backward, no matter how fast the train is moving forward!)

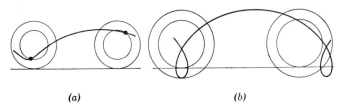

(a)   *(b)*

FIGURE 102

42. RIGID MOTIONS

Euclid's theory of congruence is predicated on the ability to move a figure from one position to another without disturbing its metric properties (e.g. length of edges, size of angles). Such motions are generally termed *rigid motions* and consist of two types or combinations of these two types. The first, called *translation*, refers to displacing a figure $\mathfrak{F}$ by allowing a fixed vector **T** to act on each point of the given figure $\mathfrak{F}$. That is, if P is a point of $\mathfrak{F}$, the point P is *translated* to Q, where

$$\overrightarrow{OQ} = \overrightarrow{OP} + \mathbf{T}. \quad \text{(See Figure 103.)}$$

The second type of rigid motion is the *rotation*, in which a figure is rotated about a fixed point in the plane. Figure 104 shows an ellipse and a triangle rotated simultaneously about the center of the ellipse.

We shall obtain analytic expressions for these rigid motions.

Suppose it is desired that the point (h, k) be moved by translation to the origin of the (x, y)-coordinate system. To keep matters straight we designate the new coordinates of a point with primes. Thus

$$(h, k) \xrightarrow{\text{translation}} (h', k') = (0, 0),$$

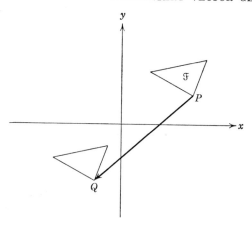

FIGURE 103

which, in terms of the definition, states that the translation vector **T** has the effect

$$h\mathbf{i} + k\mathbf{j} + \mathbf{T} = \mathbf{O}.$$

Hence $$\mathbf{T} = -h\mathbf{i} - k\mathbf{j}.$$

In general, the point (x, y) moves to point (x', y'), and

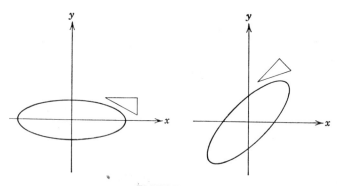

FIGURE 104

their relationship follows from the equation

$$x\mathbf{i} + y\mathbf{j} + \mathbf{T} = x'\mathbf{i} + y'\mathbf{j},$$

or $$(x - h)\mathbf{i} + (y - k)\mathbf{j} = x'\mathbf{i} + y\mathbf{j}.$$

Thus $$\begin{cases} x' = x - h \\ y' = y - k \end{cases}$$

are *the equations of translation.*

In order to discover the equations describing a rotation about the origin of the coordinate system, let $P = (x, y)$ rotate clockwise through the angle θ to its new position $P' = (x', y')$. For purposes of our analysis, let α be the angle that the position vector P makes with the positive x-axis (see Figure 105). Then

$$x = \mathbf{P} \cdot \mathbf{i} = |\mathbf{P}| \cos \alpha = |\mathbf{P}'| \cos \alpha$$
$$\text{(since } |\mathbf{P}| = |\mathbf{P}'|) \quad (123)$$
$$y = \mathbf{P} \cdot \mathbf{j} = |\mathbf{P}| \sin \alpha = |\mathbf{P}'| \sin \alpha,$$

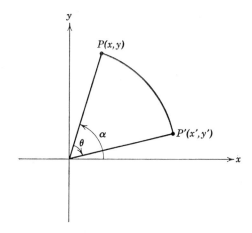

FIGURE 105

and

$$x' = \mathbf{P}' \cdot \mathbf{i} = \left|\mathbf{P}'\right| \cos(\alpha - \theta) = \left|\mathbf{P}'\right| \cos \alpha \cos \theta \qquad (124)$$
$$+ \left|\mathbf{P}'\right| \sin \alpha \sin \theta$$
$$y' = \mathbf{P}' \cdot \mathbf{j} = \left|\mathbf{P}'\right| \sin(\alpha - \theta) = \left|\mathbf{P}'\right| \sin \alpha \cos \theta$$
$$- \left|\mathbf{P}'\right| \cos \alpha \sin \theta.$$

Imposing equations (123) in the right members of (124), we arrive at

$$\begin{cases} x' = x \cos \theta + y \sin \theta \qquad (125) \\ y' = -x \sin \theta + y \cos \theta, \end{cases}$$

which analytically describes the rotation stipulated above.

EXERCISE
Rotations are usually described by a pair of equations that follow from (125) by solving for x and y. (a) Carry out this algebraic procedure. (b) Derive these equations directly by vector methods analogous to those used to determine (125).

EXAMPLE 52. Take the circle $(x - 1)^2 + (y + 2)^2 = 4$. We discuss the translation of the circle so that its new center is at the origin.

The given circle is centered at $(1, -2)$. The point $(1, -2)$ becomes the origin under the translation

$$\begin{cases} x' = x - 1 \\ y' = y + 2. \end{cases}$$

Thus, the translated circle is $x'^2 + y'^2 = 4$. Observe that the algebraic transformation did not affect the radius, which is, after all, the circle's metric property that was to remain unaltered.

EXAMPLE 53. If the points of the plane are rotated $\pi/6$ (or $30°$) clockwise, what will be the new location of the point $(1, -2)$?

The equations of the rotation through $\pi/6$ are:

$$\begin{cases} x' = x\,\dfrac{\sqrt{3}}{2} + y\,\dfrac{1}{2} \\[2mm] y' = -x\dfrac{1}{2} + y\,\dfrac{\sqrt{3}}{2} \end{cases}$$

Therefore

$$x' = \frac{\sqrt{3}}{2} - 1 = \text{approximately } -0.13$$

$$y' = -\frac{1}{2} - \sqrt{3} = \text{approximately } -2.24,$$

which states that

$$(1, -2) \xrightarrow[\text{thru } \pi/6]{\text{rotation}} (-0.13, -2.24).$$

EXERCISES

1. Find the coordinates of the point $(2, -3)$ if the translation moves the origin to

    (a) $(4, 5)$; (b) $(-3, 3)$; (c) $(-5, 4)$.

2. Find the coordinates of

    (a) $(2, 4)$; (b) $(-3, 6)$; (c) $(-2, 0)$

when the axes are rotated counterclockwise through the angle arcsin $\frac{4}{5}$.

3. Do the same as Exercise 2 when the axes are rotated counterclockwise through the angle $\pi/4$.

4. Show that the equation $x^2 + y^2 = r^2$ is unchanged by any rotation of the axes.

5. A *cylindrical surface* is generated by a line moving in such a way as to be always parallel to its original position. If, as the generating line moves, it remains perpendicular to a fixed plane and traces out a circle in the fixed plane, the cylinder is termed *right circular*.

    (a) Provide a reasonable definition for the radius of a right circular cylinder.

(b) By analogy—perhaps loose—with the cone, define *axis* for a right circular cylinder. (See the first of the Miscellaneous Exercises that follow.)

(c) Find, by vector methods, the equation of the **right** circular cylinder that cuts the xz-plane in the circle $(x - 1)^2 + (z + 1)^2 = 1$ and whose axis is parallel to the y-axis.

6. Let $P_0 = (x_0, y_0, z_0)$ be the center of a sphere that has $P_1 = (x_1, y_1, z_1)$ as one of its points. Using vector techniques, prove that
$$(x - x_0)(x_1 - x_0) + (y - y_0)(y_1 - y_0) + (z - z_0)(z_1 - z_0) = 0$$
is the equation of the plane tangent to the sphere at P_1.

MISCELLANEOUS GEOMETRIC EXERCISES

1. If a line χ varies in such a way that it always intersects a fixed line $\mathcal{L}$ in a fixed point V at an angle $\frac{1}{2}\alpha(< \pi/2)$, then χ is said to generate a *right circular cone* with axis $\mathcal{L}$, vertex V, and vertex angle α (see Figure 106).

Prove by vector methods that the right circular cone, with vertex at the origin, axis the z-axis, and vertex angle $2\pi/3$, is represented by the equation $x^2 + y^2 - 3z^2 = 0$.

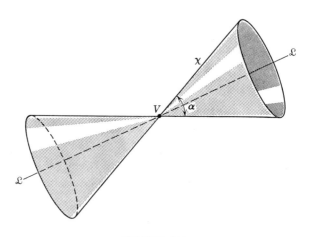

FIGURE 106

(*Hint.* Let **P** be the position vector of $P = (x, y, z)$ on the cone. Then $\mathbf{P} \cdot \mathbf{k} = |\mathbf{P}| \cos \pi/3$ is the vector equation of the cone.)

2. Find the equation that represents the cone whose axis is the x-axis, vertex is at the origin, and vertex angle is $\pi/2$.

3. Find the equation that represents the cone, whose axis is the z-axis, vertex is at $(0, 0, 2)$, and vertex angle is $2\pi/3$.

4. Given points A, B, and R in space, find a formula for the distance d from R to line AB.

(*Hint.* If $\overrightarrow{AR}$ and $\overrightarrow{AB}$ make an angle θ, then $d = |\overrightarrow{AR}| \sin \theta$; but $\sin \theta$ may be determined from $\overrightarrow{AR} \times \overrightarrow{AB}$.)

Observe that (i) the equation of line AB is never needed; and (ii) interchanging the roles of A and B yields a check.

5. Prove, by vector methods, that the area of a triangle formed by joining the midpoint of one of the nonparallel sides of a trapezoid to the endpoints of the opposite side is half that of the trapezoid.

6. Prove by vector methods: If a straight line is equally inclined to three coplanar lines, it is perpendicular to their plane.

7. Prove: The sum of the squares of the edges of any tetrahedron is equal to four times the sum of the squares of joins of the midpoints of opposite edges.

8. Find the angle between two nonintersecting edges of a regular tetrahedron.

appendix—
expansion
of
determinants

For the reader who is unfamiliar with the theory of determinants, we provide a brief description of the method of determinant expansion. This discussion does not attempt to communicate mathematical insight into theory but merely provides a mnemonic device for dealing with cross products by means of a compact notation.

The *two by two* determinant, written $\begin{vmatrix} a_1 & a_2 \\ b_1 & b_2 \end{vmatrix}$ represents a quantity according to the following expansion:

$$\begin{vmatrix} a_1 & a_2 \\ b_1 & b_2 \end{vmatrix} = a_1 b_2 - a_2 b_1.$$

The *three by three* determinant is expanded as follows:

$$\begin{vmatrix} a_1 & a_2 & a_3 \\ b_1 & b_2 & b_3 \\ c_1 & c_2 & c_3 \end{vmatrix} = a_1 \begin{vmatrix} b_2 & b_3 \\ c_2 & c_3 \end{vmatrix} - a_2 \begin{vmatrix} b_1 & b_3 \\ c_1 & c_3 \end{vmatrix}$$

$$+ a_3 \begin{vmatrix} b_1 & b_2 \\ c_1 & c_2 \end{vmatrix} = a_1 b_2 c_3 - a_1 b_3 c_2 - a_2 b_1 c_3$$

$$+ a_2 b_3 c_1 + a_3 b_1 c_2 - a_3 b_2 c_1.$$

(Observe that interchanging the second and third rows leads to an expression which is the negative of the one we have computed. This is the algebraic equivalent of $\mathbf{A} \times \mathbf{B} = -\mathbf{B} \times \mathbf{A}$.)

There are various approaches to expanding determinants, and there are several devices by which one recalls the expansion. However, the reader who is not familiar with determinants would be wise to stick to the particular expansion of cross products in this volume. In accordance with the given expansion, we view the cross product

$$(a_1\mathbf{i} + a_2\mathbf{j} + a_3\mathbf{k}) \times (b_1\mathbf{i} + b_2\mathbf{j} + b_3\mathbf{k})$$

as equal to

$$\begin{vmatrix} \mathbf{i} & \mathbf{j} & \mathbf{k} \\ a_1 & a_2 & a_3 \\ b_1 & b_2 & b_3 \end{vmatrix} = \mathbf{i} \begin{vmatrix} a_2 & a_3 \\ b_2 & b_3 \end{vmatrix} - \mathbf{j} \begin{vmatrix} a_1 & a_3 \\ b_1 & b_3 \end{vmatrix} + \mathbf{k} \begin{vmatrix} a_1 & a_2 \\ b_1 & b_2 \end{vmatrix}$$

$$= (a_2 b_3 - a_3 b_2)\mathbf{i} + (a_3 b_1 - a_1 b_3)\mathbf{j} + (a_1 b_2 - a_2 b_1)\mathbf{k}.$$

answers

SECTION 3

4. $\sqrt{89}$. **5.** $100\sqrt{2}$.

SECTION 4

5. (a) $l = \dfrac{2}{5}$, $m = \dfrac{3}{5}$. (b) $l = \dfrac{4}{7}$, $m = \dfrac{3}{7}$. (c) $l = \dfrac{5}{2}$, $m = \dfrac{-3}{2}$.

SECTION 5

5. They are equal.

SECTION 8

1. (b) $\mathbf{A} = 6\mathbf{i} + 4\mathbf{j} + 10\mathbf{k}$, $\mathbf{B} = -6\mathbf{i} + 4\mathbf{j} - 10\mathbf{k}$, $\mathbf{C} = 4\mathbf{i} - 6\mathbf{j} - 10\mathbf{k}$, $\mathbf{D} = 10\mathbf{j} + 4\mathbf{k}$. (c) $4\mathbf{i} + 12\mathbf{j} - 6\mathbf{k}$.
(d) $\mathbf{A} - \mathbf{B} = 12\mathbf{i} + 20\mathbf{k}$, $\overrightarrow{BD} = 6\mathbf{i} + 6\mathbf{j} + 14\mathbf{k}$.
(f) $(-18, 4, -30)$. (g) $(-18, 4, -30)$.
2. (a) $4\mathbf{i} - 8\mathbf{j}$. (b) $3\mathbf{i} + 6\mathbf{j}$. (c) $-7\mathbf{i} + 2\mathbf{j}$. (e) Yes. (f) Yes.
(g) $(2, -3, 3)$. **3.** No. **4.** (a) No. (b) $\mathbf{V} = \dfrac{1}{3}\mathbf{A} + \dfrac{5}{3}\mathbf{B} + \dfrac{8}{3}\mathbf{C}$.

SECTION 14

3. $\dfrac{4}{\sqrt{13}}(3\mathbf{i} + 2\mathbf{j})$ or $\dfrac{-4}{\sqrt{13}}(3\mathbf{i} + 2\mathbf{j})$. **4.** $\dfrac{\sqrt{21}}{7}$. **10.** (a) -11.

(b) $\dfrac{-11\sqrt{6}}{6}$ and $\dfrac{-11\sqrt{29}}{29}$.   (c) $\dfrac{-11}{\sqrt{29}}(2\mathbf{i}+\mathbf{j}-\mathbf{k})$.

(d) 4 units.   **11.** Because the dot product is distributive.

SECTION 16

1. (a) $\mathbf{P}=(1-t)(5\mathbf{i}+4\mathbf{j})+t(3\mathbf{i}+\mathbf{j})$.   (b) $x=5-2t$,

$y=4+5t$.   (c) $5x+2y=33$.   **2.** (a) $\dfrac{-5}{2}$.   (b) $\dfrac{33}{5},\dfrac{33}{2}$.

3. (a) $9x+5y+25=0$.   (b) $y=2x+6$.   (c) $2x-y=1$.
4. $(6,0)$.   **6.** (a) $(2,-1)$ (b) $x+3y+1=0$.
(c) $x=-2+(7\sqrt{34}+5\sqrt{58})t,\ y=1-3(\sqrt{34}+\sqrt{58})t$.
7. (a) $3y=\sqrt{3}\,x-(6+\sqrt{3})$.   (b) $x=1$.   (c) $y=-2$.
9. (c) $x=0$.

SECTION 17

1. $\mathbf{N}=a\mathbf{i}+b\mathbf{j}$.   **2.** (a) $x+2y=0$.   **3.** $x+4y=6$.

4. $\pm\dfrac{\sqrt{5}}{5}(2\mathbf{i}-\mathbf{j})$.

SECTION 18

1. $\dfrac{8}{\sqrt{5}}$.   **2.** 0.   **3.** 0.   **4.** 0.   **5.** $\dfrac{11}{5}$.

SECTION 19

6. $\tan\theta=\dfrac{m_2-m_1}{1+m_1m_2}$.   **8.** (a) arc $\tan\dfrac{25}{9}$, arc $\tan\dfrac{9}{25},\dfrac{\pi}{2}$.

9. $-7\pm\sqrt{50}$.   **10.** $y=\dfrac{5\sqrt{3}+9\sqrt{2}}{9}\,x$.   **12.** $x-8y=0$.

13. (a) $m(x-1)+n(y-2)=0$.   (b) $y=\dfrac{\sqrt{3}}{3}x+b$.

14. (a) $5x+4y-2=0$.   (b) $7x-32y-3=0$.

SECTION 20

1. (a) $x^2+(y-1)^2=4$.   (b) $x^2+(y+1)^2=4$.
(c) $(x+2)^2+(y-3)^2=9$.   **2.** (a) $(x-2)^2+(y+1)^2=5$.

(b) $5x^2+5y^2-\frac{1}{5}x-\frac{9}{5}y-\dfrac{18}{5}=0$.

(c) $x^2+y^2-8x+12y=0$.   **3.** (a) $(8,-6)$.

10. (d) $\left(-\dfrac{4}{3}, \dfrac{2}{3}\right), \dfrac{\sqrt{65}}{3}.$ **4.** (a) $3x + 4y = 24.$

7. (a) $9x + 2y = 40.$ (c) $y = -x + 2\sqrt{2}.$

9. (a) $x = -1 + 5\cos\theta,\ y = 2 + 5\cos\theta.$

(b) $x = 1 + \frac{1}{6}\sqrt{141}\ \theta,\ y = -\dfrac{3}{2} + \dfrac{1}{6}\sqrt{141}\ \theta.$

10. (a) $(1, 0)$ and $(0, 1).$ (b) $(1, 0)$ and $(0, 1).$

SECTION 21

1. (a) $\dfrac{4}{5\sqrt{2}}, \dfrac{3}{5\sqrt{2}}, \dfrac{1}{5\sqrt{2}}.$ (c) $0, 0, 1.$ (d) $0, 1, 0.$

2. (a) $(0, 1, 0),\ 1.$ **3.** (a) $(x - 1)^2 + (y + 1)^2 + z^2 = 4.$
(c) $x^2 + y^2 + z^2 = 144.$

4. (a) $3, 1, -1$ and $3m, m, -m\ (m \neq 0).$

SECTION 24

2. (a) $6x + 4y + 7z = 17.$ (c) $2x - y - z = 0.$

(e) $4x - 3y + 12z = 76.$ **3.** (a) $\dfrac{19}{13}.$ (c) $\dfrac{88}{5}.$

SECTION 26

1. (a) Two-point form is non-existent in this case. The line is given by $x = -4,\ y = 1.$ (c) Again, two-point form is non-existent. Line is given by $\dfrac{x + 4}{3 + 4} = \dfrac{z + 2}{2 + 2}$ and $y = 1.$

(e) $\dfrac{x - 3}{3 - 2} = \dfrac{y - 2}{2 - 10} = \dfrac{z + 5}{-5 + 9}$ and $\dfrac{x - 3}{3 - 2} = \dfrac{y - 2}{2 - 10} = \dfrac{z + 5}{-5 + 1}$

(g) $\dfrac{x - 0}{5 - 0} = \dfrac{y - 0}{-4 - 0} = \dfrac{z - 0}{6 - 0}.$ **2.** (b) $x = -4 + 9t,$
$y = 1 + 2t,\ z = -2 + t.$ (c) $x = 3 + 3t,\ y = 2 - 2t,$
$z = -5 - 6t.$ (f) $x = -4 + 3t,\ y = 1 + 4t,\ z = -2 + 12t.$

4. (a) $6, 2, 3.$ **5.** (b) $x = -\dfrac{34}{7} + 20t,\ y = -\dfrac{39}{14} + 18t,$

$z = t$ **7.** $(-12, 4, -1).$ **8.** $\dfrac{-12}{\sqrt{181}}, \dfrac{6}{\sqrt{181}}, \dfrac{1}{\sqrt{181}}.$

SECTION 28

1. In order to have $\dfrac{\pi}{2} - \beta$ be first quadrant angle.

3. $(9, -5, 12)$. **5.** $\left(-\dfrac{33}{10}, -\dfrac{69}{20}, -\dfrac{39}{20} \right)$, $\sin \beta = \dfrac{8}{21}$.

6. (a) Use vectors normal to the planes. (c) $\cos \theta = \dfrac{13}{\sqrt{45}}$.

8. (a) $\cos \theta = \dfrac{1}{\sqrt{3}}$. (c) $\sin \beta = \dfrac{1}{\sqrt{3}}$

SECTION 32

1. (a) $\mathbf{k} - \mathbf{j}$. (c) $\mathbf{O}$. (e) $8\mathbf{j} - 4\mathbf{k}$. **2.** Use triple scalar product.

6. (b) $x + y + z = 1$. **7.** $d = \left| \mathbf{A} - \dfrac{\overrightarrow{AB} \times \overrightarrow{AC}}{|\overrightarrow{AB} \times \overrightarrow{AC}|} \right|$. **9.** (a) 0.

(c) $\dfrac{2}{3}$. **11.** $b_1 c_2 - b_2 c_1,\ a_2 c_1 - a_1 c_2,\ a_1 b_2 + a_2 b_1$.

SECTION 33

2. $-13\mathbf{i} - 7\mathbf{j} + 5\mathbf{k}$. **6.** $\mathbf{A} \times \mathbf{B}$ and $\mathbf{C} \times \mathbf{D}$ are parallel. Hence their cross product is the zero vector.

SECTION 36

2. (a) Annular region centered at origin (including the bounding circles. (b) Spherical shell including the bounding spheres. **3.** A torus (doughnut) whose circular cross-section has a radius of one. **4.** (a) $4 < x^2 + y^2 < 9$.
(b) $0 < x < 1$ and $1 - x < y < x + 1$.

SECTION 38

4. If $ABCD$ is a tetrahedron or a square then $\mathbf{X} = r_1\mathbf{A} + r_2\mathbf{B} + r_3\mathbf{C} + r_4\mathbf{D}$, with $0 \leq r_i \leq 1$ and $r_1 + r_2 + r_3 + r_4 = 1$.

5. At least one coefficient equals zero. **9.** (a) $\left(\dfrac{2}{3}, \dfrac{2}{3} \right)$,

$\mathbf{M} = \frac{1}{3}\mathbf{A} + \frac{1}{3}\mathbf{B} + \frac{1}{3}\mathbf{C}$. (b) $(1, 1)$.
10. (a) $\mathbf{X} = r_1\mathbf{A} + r_2\mathbf{B} + r_3\mathbf{C}$, with $0 \leq r_i \leq 1$ and $r_1 + r_2 + r_3 = 1$. (c) Insist that $0 < r_i < 1$.

SECTION 39

1. (*a*) Note that $m + s + b = 500$ for maximum profit.
(*b*) 100 milk, 300 semi-sweet, 100 bitter.
2. max = 7, min = 5.   **3.** 400 gal regular, 300 gal high test, 300 gal white.   **4.** 800 gal regular, 200 gal high test.
5. $\frac{2}{3}$ *A*-ration,   4 *B*-ration.

SECTION 41

2. (*a*) $x = r\theta - a \sin \theta, y = r - a \cos \theta$.
(*b*) $x = r\theta - a \sin \theta, y = r - a \cos \theta$.

SECTION 42

1. (*a*) $(6, 2)$.   (*c*) $(-3, 1)$.   **2.** (*a*) $\left(\dfrac{21}{5}, \dfrac{4}{5}\right)$.   (*c*) $\left(\dfrac{-6}{5}, \dfrac{-8}{5}\right)$.
5. (*c*) $(x - 1)^2 + (z + 1)^2 = 1$.

MISCELLANEOUS EXERCISES

2. $x^2 = y^2 + z^2$.   **3.** $3(z - 2)^2 = x^2 + y^2$.
4. $d = \dfrac{\left|\overrightarrow{AR} \times \overrightarrow{AB}\right|}{\left|\overrightarrow{AB}\right|}$.   **8.** $\dfrac{\pi}{2}$.

index

Absolute value, 14, 57–9
Addition of vectors, 9, 11–13
Altitudes, 75
Auxiliary point technique, 30
Axioms, 1

Basis, 46–9
Bisectors, perpendicular, 66–7
Bound vector, 9
Bypass lemma, 19

Circle, 100 ff.
Commutativity, 9, 63, 187
Complex plane, 54–9
Components, 68–70, 73
Cone, 202
Convexity, 167–9
Coordinate-free methods, 76
Coplanar vectors, 27, 34
Courant, R., 181
Coxeter, H. S. M., 181
Cross product, 135 ff.
    triple, 147–50

Curate cycloid, 196
Cycloid, 191–3
    Curate, 196
    Prolate, 196
Cylinder, 201

Deductive science, 1
Dependence, 21 ff.
Desargues' theorem, 181 ff., 188,
    191
Determinants, 141, appendix
Dimension, 49
Direction angles, 108
Direction cosines, 108–10, 125
Direction numbers, 110–1, 123–5
Distance, 60–1
Distributivity, 65, 139
Division of segments, 27–9, 34
Dodecahedron, 54
Dot product, 62 ff.

Equilibrium, 10, 20

Force, 7–8, 10, 20, 73
Free vector, 6–7, 9

Galileo, 11
Generates (= spans), 48
Great circle, 157

Hall, D. W., 19
Hero's formula, 156
Hilbert, David, 187

"If and only if", 6
Incidence, 180, 185
Inclination, angle of, 81
Inner product, 60 ff.
Intercept form, 87
Inverse, additive, 16
Involute, 193–6

Klamkin, Murray S., 148

Lagrange, identity of, 150
Law of cosines, 150, 158
Law of sines, 150–1, 158–9
Left-handed triple, 43 ff.
Lichtenberg, Donovan, 170
Line of action, 7–8
Linear programming, 170 ff.
Length, 57–9
Linear combination, 20–21, 35
Linear dependence, 21 ff.

Mechanics, 7–8, 10, 68–9, 73
Menelaus theorem, 188–90
Model, 3
Multiplication by scalar, 12 ff.

Negative triple, 43 ff.
Newman, J. R., 53

Ordered set, 43
Orientation, 40 ff.

Pappus' theorem, 185, 188, 191
Parallelism, 86

Parallel postulate, 2
Parameter, 78
Parametric representation, 78–
    80, 122, 146, 191
Pencil of lines, 100
Perpendicularity, 63, 89
Planes, 111 ff.
Point-slope form, 87
Position vector, 46, 49
Positive triple, 43 ff.
Postulate, parallel, 2
Postulates, 1
Programming, linear, 170 ff.
Projection, 64–6
Projective geometry, 180 ff.
Prolate cycloid, 196
Pyramid, 146

Radial vectors, 52–4, 56
Radians, 43
Resultant, 10, 20
Rhombus, 156–7
Right-handed triple, 43 ff.
Rigid motions, 197–201
Robbins, H., 181
Rotation, 197, 199–201

Scalar, 4–5
Scalar, product, 63 ff.
    triple, 137–43
Segment division, 27–9, 34
Set theory, 21, 35, 85, 165, 167
Shortcut lemma, 19
Slope, 81
Slope-intercept form, 83
Space, 49
Span, 48
Sphere, 106 ff.
    unit, 108–10
Statics, 10
Staudt, K. G. C. von, 187
Stevin, Simon, 10, 11
Straight line, 77 ff., 121 ff.

Subtraction, 16–17
Symmetry, 53

Terminus (= endpoint), 5, 9
Traces, 114–15
Translation, 197–9
Triple cross product, 147–50
Triple scalar product, 137–43
Trochoid, 196
Two-point form, 80, 126

Union, 167
Uniqueness of representation, 34 ff.
Unit sphere, 108
Unit vector, 5

Vector(s), addition of, 9, 11–13
  bound, 9
  definition of, 4
  direction of, 4, 6, 13

Vector(s), equality of, 6, 10
  free, 6–7, 9
  line of action of, 7–8
  linear combinations of, 20 ff., 35
  linear dependence of, 21 ff.
  magnitude of, 4, 6
  multiplication by scalar, 12 ff.
  origin of, 6
  radial, 52–3
  subtraction of, 7, 16
  sum of, 9
  unit, 5
  zero, 5, 12, 14, 22
Vector product, 136 ff.
Vector product, triple, 147–50

Weyl, Hermann, 53
Work, 73

Zero vector, 5, 12, 14, 22
Zweng, Marilyn, 170